The Institute of Chartered Financial Analysts
Continuing Education Series

Analyzing Investment Opportunities in Distressed and Bankrupt Companies

September 11, 1990
Chicago, Illinois

Edward I. Altman
David J. Breazzano
James A. Gentry
Shelley F. Greenhaus
Paul S. Levy
Roger F. Murray

Frank K. Reilly, CFA
James E. Spiotto
Dean J. Takahashi
Jeffrey I. Werbalowsky
Richard S. Wilson

Edited by
Thomas A. Bowman, CFA

Sponsored by the
Association for Investment
Management and Research

Additional copies of this publication may be ordered from:

Association for Investment Management and Research
P.O. Box 7947
Charlottesville, VA 22906
1-804-977-5724 (Phone)
1-804-977-0350 (Fax)

The Association for Investment Management and Research
comprises the Institute of Chartered Financial Analysts and
the Financial Analysts Federation.

Katrina F. Sherrerd, CFA, *Managing Editor*
Joni L. Tomal, *Associate Editor*
Diane B. Hamshar, *Typesetting/Layout*

ISBN 1-879087-06-5

Printed in the United States of America

2/15/91

Table of Contents

Foreword

Although the existence of securities of distressed and bankrupt companies is certainly not a recent phenomenon, the decade of the 1980s witnessed the highest corporate bond default rates of this century. The significant increase in leveraged buyouts and corporate mergers, financed primarily through the issuance of high-yield or junk bonds, was a major factor in pushing the current market value of distressed securities to approximately $200 billion versus $15 billion in 1980.

As a result of a quality orientation on the part of many institutional investors in combination with the lack of a defined discipline for analyzing distressed securities, a "flight to quality" has caused major inefficiencies to occur in the market values of these securities. As Roger Murray points out in the Overview, not only must the investor understand the need for detailed credit analysis, but other legal, tax and corporate structure considerations must also be considered. The investor who has both a good understanding of all these issues and the discipline with which to approach the analytical process can sometimes achieve returns far in excess of more traditional asset classes such as common stocks and higher-rated fixed-income securities.

The topic of analyzing distressed and bankrupt companies was addressed at an AIMR-sponsored seminar entitled "Analyzing Investment Opportunities in Distressed and Bankrupt Companies," held in Chicago on September 11, 1990. These proceedings, which result from that seminar, provide a valuable source of information on the characteristics of the market for these securities, the key issues that must be employed in their valuation, and techniques that are employed by professionals who are actively engaged in this specialized field.

The Association for Investment Management and Research wishes to extend its sincere appreciation to the impressive group of experts who served as seminar speakers and assisted in the publication of these proceedings. Special thanks are extended to Roger F. Murray, Professor Emeritus of Finance at Columbia University's Graduate School of Business, who acted as both moderator and speaker and who provided the vision for developing a seminar on this important topic. Other speakers included James E. Spiotto, Esq., Chapman and Cutler; James A. Gentry, University of Illinois, Urbana-Champaign; Frank K. Reilly, CFA, University of Notre Dame, who also provided significant assistance in developing this seminar; Richard S. Wilson, Fitch Investors Service, Inc.; Edward I. Altman, New York University; Jeffrey I. Werbalowsky, Houlihan, Lokey, Howard & Zukin Capital; Shelley Greenhaus, Oppenheimer Horizon Partners & Company; Paul S. Levy, Lancer Industries, Inc.; David J. Breazzano, T. Rowe Price Recovery Fund Associates, Inc.; and Dean J. Takahashi, Yale University. We also thank Cary J. Stanford of Houlihan, Lokey, Howard & Zukin Capital for his contribution to this publication.

Other individuals who played an invaluable role in the seminar and the publication of these proceedings include Susan D. Martin, CFA, Vice President of AIMR, who organized the seminar, and Katrina F. Sherrerd, CFA, Vice President of AIMR, who, with her excellent editorial staff, greatly assisted me in the editing of this publication.

Thomas A. Bowman, CFA
Executive Vice President
Association for Investment
Management and Research

Biographies of Speakers

Edward I. Altman is the Max L. Heine Professor of Finance and Chairman of the M.B.A. Program at the Graduate School of Business Administration at New York University. He has served as a visiting professor at several universities overseas; has been a consultant to several government agencies, financial and accounting institutions, and industrial companies; has lectured to executives in the United States and abroad; and has testified before the U.S. Congress. Dr. Altman is the editor of the *Journal of Banking and Finance* and the *Wiley Professional Banking and Finance Series*. He is the author of over 70 journal articles and numerous books, most recently *Corporate Financial Distress, Recent Advances in Corporate Finance*, and *Investing in Junk Bonds: Inside the High Yield Debt Market*.

David J. Breazzano is a Portfolio Manager at Fidelity Investments, emphasizing investments in high-yield and bankrupt securities and claims. Formerly, he was president of T. Rowe Price Recovery Fund Associates, Inc. Prior to joining T. Rowe Price, Mr. Breazzano was employed as a vice president and senior credit analyst at First Investors Asset Management and as an assistant vice president, investment research, at New York Life Insurance Company. He is currently a director of RAPCO, Inc. (Reorganized Argo Petroleum Company), and has served as chairman of creditors' committees in the following bankruptcies: Transcontinental Energy, Continental Airlines, MGF Oil, Radice, and Texas General Resources. Mr. Breazzano holds a B.A. from Union College and an M.B.A. from Cornell University.

James A. Gentry is the IBE Distinguished Professor of Finance at the College of Commerce and Business Administration of the University of Illinois at Urbana-Champaign. He joined the faculty in 1966. From 1975-79, he served as associate dean of the College of Commerce and Business Administration. He is the author of several articles on predicting bankruptcy, bond ratings and loan risks, and teaches one of the few courses in the United States that focuses exclusively on the management of working capital. He recently developed a series of cases on computerized cash management and is writing a textbook on short-run financial management. The recipient of several teaching awards, Dr. Gentry is president of the Illinois State Universities Retirement System, a director of the University of Illinois Athletic Association, and past president of the Midwest Finance Association. Dr. Gentry holds an A.B. from Indiana State University and M.B.A. and D.B.A. degrees from Indiana University.

Shelley Greenhaus, previously a senior vice president and portfolio manager at Oppenheimer Horizon Partners & Co. (Opco), is forming a money management firm specializing in troubled company investing. While at Opco, Mr. Greenhaus worked on various merger transactions for Opco and affiliated companies and consulted with corporate clients on reorganization strategies, including exchange offers, bankruptcies, and recapitalizations. Since 1983, he has managed a proprietary firm trading account that specializes in troubled-company investing. Prior to joining Opco, Mr. Greenhaus served as a financial advisor and money manager specializing in corporate reorganization, liquidations, and special situations for the William Rosenwald family (one of the founders of Sears, Roebuck & Co.) in its private investment banking group. Mr. Greenhaus holds a B.A. from York College (City University of New York) and an M.B.A. from New York University.

Paul S. Levy is Chairman and Chief Executive Officer of Lancer Industries, which he and his partners have been managing since July 1989. Lancer Industries and Joseph, Littlejohn & Levy are in the process of raising an investment partnership to invest in troubled companies. Lancer is the successor to McLean Industries, which filed for bankruptcy protection in 1986 and emerged in 1989 with an innovative structure. Prior to joining Lancer, Mr. Levy was a managing director at Drexel Burnham Lambert, where he led Drexel's restructuring group in New York. Mr. Levy holds a B.A. from Lehigh University and a J.D. from the University of Pennsylvania.

Roger F. Murray is the S. Sloan Colt Professor Emeritus of Banking and Finance at Columbia University Business School. Previously, he directed credit analysis, investment research, economics, and institutional investment advisory services at Bankers Trust Company. He also served six years as executive vice president of Teacher's Insurance and Annuity Association and the College Retirement Equities Fund. Dr. Murray is the principal architect of The Common Fund. He was a director and trustee of a number of the Alliance Capital, Eberstadt, and Putnum groups of mutual funds. He is coauthor of *Graham and Dodd's Security Analysis*, Fifth Edition (1988). He is a past president of the American Finance Association.

Frank K. Reilly, CFA, is Bernard J. Hank Professor of Business Administration at the College of Business Administration of the University of Notre Dame, and was dean of that college from 1981 to 1987. Prior to 1981, he was professor of finance at the University of Illinois at Urbana-Champaign. He was included in the list of Outstanding Educators in America and received the Alumni "Excellence in Graduate Teaching" Award, and the Outstanding Educator Award from the M.B.A. class at the University of Illinois (1981) and University of Notre Dame (1989). He is the author of *Investment Analysis and Portfolio Management* and *Investments*, as well as numerous articles in journals such as the *Journal of Portfolio Management*, *Financial Analysts Journal*, *Journal of Finance*, and *Financial Management*. Dr. Reilly holds a Ph.D. from the University of Chicago.

James E. Spiotto, Esq., is a Partner in the law firm of Chapman and Cutler. He has represented issuers, indenture trustees, or bondholders in litigation, bankruptcy, or workouts of over 300 troubled bond issues in over 35 states. He has lectured before various academic institutions, professional associations, authorities, and governmental bodies concerning the rights and remedies of bondholders and issuers regarding defaulted debt securities. Recently he has been involved in representing bondholders in exchange offers, debt restructurings, and bankruptcies related to high-yield securities. Mr. Spiotto testified before the United States Senate and House Judiciary Committees in conjunction with the recently enacted amendments to the Bankruptcy Code. He has written numerous books on troubled-debt financing, and he has just completed the treatise, *Defaulted Securities: The Prudent Indenture Trustee's Guide*. Mr. Spiotto is a graduate of the University of Chicago Law School.

Dean J. Takahashi is Director of Endowment Management for Yale University, where he oversees the management of Yale's domestic, foreign, and private equity portfolios. In addition, he is responsible for the analysis and maintenance of asset allocation policy for the university's endowment and staff pension plan. Mr. Takahashi is a director of Nicholas-Applegate Growth Equity Fund, Inc., and a member of the Highland Capital Partners Advisory Committee. He holds a B.A. in economics and an M.B.A. in public and private management from Yale University.

Jeffrey I. Werbalowsky is National Managing Director of Houlihan, Lokey, Howard & Zukin's Financial Restructuring Group, providing financial advisory and investment banking services to debtors, bondholders, and creditors' committees and the various parties in out-of-court and Chapter 11 restructurings. Previously, Mr. Werbalowsky was associated with Gibson, Dunn & Crutcher in their bankruptcy practice group from 1982 through 1985 and with Levene & Eisenberg, specializing exclusively in bankruptcy and corporate reorganization, from 1985 to 1987. In 1987 he left the law to become chief executive officer of Cheviot Capital Corporation, an investment firm engaged in transactions involving bankruptcy and distressed situations. Cheviot Capital was purchased by Houlihan, Lokey, Howard & Zukin Capital in 1988, at which time he assumed his present position. He belongs to a variety of organizations relating to bankruptcy and reorganization, and is on the editorial board of the *California Bankruptcy Journal*. Mr. Werbalowsky holds a B.A. in economics from the University of Virginia and a J.D. from Columbia University.

Richard S. Wilson is the Director of Research Products and Services at Fitch Investors Service, Inc. Before joining Fitch in May 1989, he was a first vice president and manager of domestic taxable fixed-income research at Merrill Lynch Capital Markets. He came to Merrill Lynch in 1978 as a result of the merger with White, Weld & Co., Incorporated, where he headed corporate bond research activities since 1975. His experience in fixed-income research includes senior analyst positions at other Wall Street firms as well as Standard & Poor's Corporation. Mr. Wilson is the author of *Corporate Senior Securities: Analysis and Evaluation of Bonds, Convertibles and Preferreds*, and coauthor of *The New Corporate Bond Market* with Frank Fabozzi. He is the author of several articles on corporate bond topics and has contributed to several books on the subject. He is a member of The New York Society of Security Analysts, Inc., a trustee and past director of The Financial Management Association, and a founding member and past president of the Fixed Income Analysts Society (New York). Mr. Wilson holds a B.S. in economics from the Wharton School of Finance of the University of Pennsylvania and an M.S. from the Graduate School of Business of Columbia University.

Overview of the Seminar

Roger F. Murray
S. Sloan Colt Professor Emeritus of Banking and Finance
Columbia University Business School

In Search of a Discipline

The attraction of investment opportunities in distressed and bankrupt companies remains and will persist because this is a classic case of an inefficient market. Not only is the marketplace fallible in its ability to predict deterioration in creditworthiness of debt instruments and potential risk of default, but there are nonfinancial factors, legal and regulatory for example, at work to dilute the reliability of even the best financial analysis. Because regulators usually require financial institutions to mark debt instruments to severely depressed market prices upon their default, there is no incentive to defer liquidation. History records the fact that among the highest return assets available for investment are bonds purchased at or shortly after the time of default.

The rewards and penalties for investment decisions in this asset class are magnified by the volatility and illiquidity of markets. Diversification across economic and industry sectors is not easy, and the important portfolio safeguard of diversification across time is even more difficult because of the lumpiness of opportunities and calamities. The development of a disciplined approach to the management of portfolios of such securities is sufficiently demanding to call for the kind of serious study exemplified by the topics and speakers of this seminar.

There may be three major aspects of such a discipline: (1) the analysis and valuation of individual companies and their securities, (2) the construction of the portfolio of distressed and bankrupt company securities that diversifies away some critical elements of specific risk, and (3) the development of a rationale for the inclusion of quantities of such assets in portfolios. From different perspectives, these elements of a disciplined approach are addressed by our very able panel of experts.

Understanding Insolvency

The substantial similarities between a corporate restructuring and a bankruptcy reorganization are identified by James Spiotto in explaining how the long delays and expenses of the bankruptcy process can be greatly reduced by the negotiation of a prepackaged plan. But before any such solution can be reached, he emphasizes, it is necessary to determine whether the business is really viable on an operating basis. If such is not the case, liquidation under Chapter 7 may be the most expeditious process. If financial rather than operating problems have produced insolvency, however, Chapter 11 reorganizations can be the answer. Fundamental analysis has its specific role in reaching such conclusions.

A new and not completely resolved issue among the traditional legal aspects of the reorganization process is the question of whether a leveraged buyout could be considered a fraudulent coneyance. This is, of course, only one item in the extensive checklist that Spiotto provides of the legal considerations that must be understood in making an investment commitment and perhaps protecting it through a period of insolvency.

Estimating Cash Flows

The analysis of cash flows provides a sound basis for evaluating the financial strengths and health of corporations as operating entities. The level and variability of free cash flows, therefore, are the indicators of actual or potential distress presented by James Gentry. This type of analysis of financial statements systematically examines the economics of the business and the capacity of management to direct resources to productive opportunities.

Using Cash Flows and Financial Ratios to Predict Bankruptcies

In his presentation, Frank Reilly gives us a comprehensive view of bankruptcy prediction models, which are based on financial ratios. He observes that cash flow and financial ratio models are complementary. He also notes that the addition of a measure of corporate liquidity enhances both kinds of models. Reilly's excellent analysis of different approaches also reminds us that investors in distressed securities can track the same variables to observe progress and

1

to predict possible recovery from financial difficulties.

Covenants: What Kind of Protection Do They Offer?

The issue of whether covenants significantly protect investors is addressed by Richard Wilson. Although strong covenants cannot make a weak credit strong, their absence has frequently produced the opposite result. A protracted inattention to bond indenture terms may be giving way to new assertions of bondholder rights, especially in light of the recent wave of restructurings and bankruptcies. Covenants are being reviewed and negotiated with increased emphasis.

The Market for Distressed and Defaulted Securities

The size of the market for distressed and defaulted securities is well in excess of $200 billion and still growing, according to Edward Altman's estimates. Of this total, perhaps $5 billion is under active management by firms with a commitment to distressed securities investing. Rates of recoveries and returns suggest that good credit analysis pays. For recent years, a defaulted bond index shows a low correlation, only 25 percent, with the S&P 500, suggesting that a strong diversification potential may exist.

Evaluating Distressed Securities: A Case Study

We are reminded by Jeffrey Werbalowsky that if distress is truly an operating problem, financial restructuring is no solution. But if the distress is from excessive financial leveraging, a good solution may be found by scaling down the various claimants to a realistic value of the enterprise. Such an exercise is presented in the form of a case of distress created by a shortfall from LBO projections. The restructuring presents a rationale for the treatment of each class of security.

Active Versus Passive Approaches to Investing in Distressed Securities

Paul Levy, in presenting the case for active approaches, defines the team and talents needed to deal with operating as well as financial problems in a distressed company. His team is expected to provide capital while leading the workout process. Passive approaches, as described by Shelley Greenhaus, simply seek to take advantage of the severe depreciation in price of claims against distressed companies. Ultimately, positions may require an active participation in the workout, but the passive investor seeks to avoid being an insider until the restructuring is at hand. Both active and passive participants need to observe the extent to which the absolute priority rule may be operative in the restructuring.

Case Histories: Success Versus Failure—The Advantage of Hindsight

The Public Service Company of New Hampshire bankruptcy was a complicated, unprecedented situation and, as a consequence, proved to afford an exceptionally good investment opportunity. It is the success example presented by David Breazzano. In contrast, he reports on the Liquor Barn bankruptcy, in which unfortunate business decisions produced substantial losses even to senior creditors. Once again, operating rather than financial decisions proved to be critical.

The Institutional Investor Perspective

A different perspective on investing in the securities of distressed companies is that of the institution employing outside managers. Dean Takahashi reports on the Yale University endowment's activities through three managers. The selection and monitoring of such managers became, of course, the principal tasks of the university's investment staff. An opportunistic approach guides the size of the allocation to this sector, with a present potential of up to 3 percent of total assets in a highly equity-oriented mix.

A Seminar Theme

Given the sensitivity of potential returns to economic, financial, and capital market environments, the experts are not coming up with a target percentage for allocation to securities of bankrupt and distressed companies. Legal, regulatory, accounting, tax, and ownership factors all affect the timing and success of restructuring efforts. Opportunism, then, is given preference over any secular asset allocation decision.

Because financial engineering frequently proves to be an inadequate substitute for operating managerial skills, all of us as financial analysts must be wary of possible repetitions of the kinds of mistakes that created the present huge volume of investment opportunities in distressed situations. When the full record of this period lies before us, space for the recounting of outstanding successes will be shared with the numerous cases where the verdict was correctly "the first loss was the best loss."

Understanding Insolvency

James E. Spiotto[1]
Chapman and Cutler

The bankruptcy process offers one of the best examples of an inefficient market. A bankruptcy can waste time, money, and effort, and it can destroy value more quickly than any other mechanism. People are getting better at trying to understand the process that exists and opportunities presented during a bankruptcy.

To analyze investment possibilities in distressed and bankrupt companies, an investor must understand the bankruptcy and reorganization processes, workouts, debt restructurings, and relevant tax issues. This presentation includes an overview of the bankruptcy and workout processes and then focuses on the current issues affecting them.

Default History

The annual default rate on corporate bonds has varied significantly in this century: Between the Great Depression years of 1930 and 1933 the default rate was 1.7 percent; between 1944 and 1965 it was less than 0.5 percent; and in many years it was less than 0.1 percent. For example, between 1966 and 1977 corporate bond defaults amounted to about $2 billion; during 1987, in contrast, corporate bond defaults exceeded $9 billion—in one year, defaults were four times as great as during the entire period of 1966 to 1977. That period included the banner year of 1970, in which Penn Central Railroad went into bankruptcy; a default of this magnitude was unthinkable just three years earlier.

The data indicate a trend toward more defaults and more problems. Because of the type of financing that occurred in the late 1970s and 1980s and the advent of high-yield bonds, today we are experiencing a higher default rate. One recent study indicated that between 1979 and June of 1990, over $214 billion worth of high-yield debt was issued. Of this amount, $26 billion actually went into default—an average

default rate of over 3 percent per year. The losses on the $26 billion were approximately $16 billion. Noteworthy is the fact that 83 percent of the high-yield defaults during this period occurred within the past three and a half years.[2]

Bankruptcy History

The statistics on bankruptcy are similar to those on default. In 1989 the number of companies that filed for bankruptcy was five times greater than in 1950. During the mid-1980s, there were more bankruptcies per year than in any year during the Great Depression. **Figure 1** shows total business bankruptcy filings for the years 1980 to 1989, with details on the number of Chapter 7 (liquidations), Chapter 11 (reorganizations), Chapter 12 (farmers), and Chapter 13 (individuals) bankruptcies. The peaks correspond to downturns in the economy, which are generally followed by a rise in the number of bankruptcies. An upturn in the number of bankruptcies occurs with a delay after the peak years of the downturn. If people are correct in assuming that we are headed toward deeper economic problems, then this theory suggests that there will be a significant increase in the number of bankruptcies.

The subgroup filing patterns are not highly correlated. The pattern of Chapter 7 filings and total filings is highly correlated; the correlation between Chapter 11 filings and total filings is considerably less so. Chapter 11 filings normally do not increase at a high rate as do the total filings. Often a reorganization under Chapter 11 will become a Chapter 7 liquidation. The correlation between Chapter 12 and Chapter 13 filings is not as high as the correlation between Chapter 7 and Chapter 11 filings.

The Reorganization Process

To obtain bankruptcy protection, a company must be insolvent. Legally, insolvency exists when liabilities exceed assets and a company or individual cannot

---

[2]*Original Issue High Yield Default Study*, September 6, 1990. New York: Salomon Brothers Inc.

Figure 1. U.S. Business Bankruptcy Filings (1980-89)

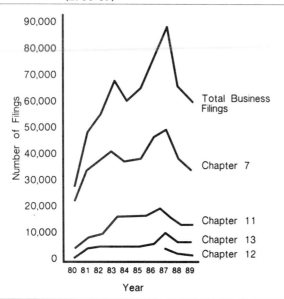

Source: Statistics obtained from the Annual Report of the Director of the Administrative Office of the United States Courts. The chart was created by the author.

pay debts as they come due. The filings by Texaco and others, however, show that insolvency may be brought about by off-balance-sheet liabilities or lawsuits that cause a company to be unable to pay maturing debts.

In addition to the company itself filing for bankruptcy, any three creditors who have liquidated claims in aggregate of more than $5,000 also can file. In the past, trade creditors have been the ones to force these bankruptcy filings. Occasionally institutional bondholders have threatened to start bankruptcy proceedings, and have done so. In general, however, either the company files voluntarily or trade creditors force the bankruptcy. In the case of a workout (debt restructuring outside of bankruptcy), the parties involved generally attempt to keep everyone calm and try to avoid bankruptcy. Whether peace can in fact be maintained is always a difficult question. Calmness depends on the flow of information and the assurance that things will work out.

Once a bankruptcy petition is filed, the reorganization process begins. The steps of a reorganization process are illustrated in **Exhibit 1**.[3] Investment professionals must analyze several areas: the company's financial condition, the projections for the company and its industry, the legal considera-

---

[3]Exhibits 1-6 and Tables 1-2 have been adapted from the treatise, written by James E. Spiotto, *Default Securities: The Prudent Indenture Trustee's Guide*, published by the American Bankers Association in June of 1990. The book contains a more extensive discussion of these related topics.

tions, the priority of claims, and the structure of the reorganization plan.

Financial Condition

The first step is to analyze the company's financial condition. Public debtholders or investors should determine the viability and feasibility of the underlying business. In analyzing a bankrupt company, the main concern is to find out where the bleeding is occurring. Identifying the bleeding and stopping it are the first steps toward being able to think about reorganization. Most bankruptcies are a result of one or more of the following factors: the industry is dead; the company has not supplied a product or service that is of value to anyone; the company overspent, overprojected, or misjudged a situation; or the company has been subject to a rash of lawsuits for environmental or pension reasons. If the business is dead, it should be buried before the stench becomes too great. It is contrary to the best interests of the holders and the indenture trustee to try to breathe life into a dead carcass.

If the company is the proverbial buggy-whip maker with a market niche that no longer exists, there is probably no point in trying to rejuvenate the company. Sometimes, there are companies that just die, and the harder people try to resuscitate them, the worse it gets for everyone. That is the most difficult thing to recognize. For these companies, the advantage in bankruptcy is the ability to liquidate quickly. The analyst needs to look at the projections for the company and examine the business itself to determine if liquidation is the best alternative. The following questions must be addressed:

- Is the company faltering because of specific problems in the business itself (for example, poor management) or because of a general downturn in the economy or business cycle?
- Is the industry faced with increasing foreign competition?
- Is the company slow to respond to technological change?
- Is the industry currently fragmented and moving toward consolidation?
- Where are the company and its products postured within the industry and in relation to peers?

The company's cash producers and cash users must be identified. Debt financing has been famous in the past few years as a way of providing for bankrupt companies' cash needs. Although some attempts have been successful, companies still have difficulty borrowing significant amounts of money. Few institutions will lend to troubled companies, so many of these companies cannot get the financing

Exhibit 1. Overview of the Reorganization Process

```
                              ┌─────────────────┐
                              │   Bankruptcy    │
                              └─────────────────┘
```

Analyze the Company's Financial Condition

- Preparation of Debtor Projections
- Review of Debtor Projections for the following:
  - Optional cash flow for distribution
  - Business strategies for core assets
  - Credit and other financial techniques
  - Proceeds from sale of nonoperating assets (noncore)
  - Corporate general and administrative expenses and capital expenditures
- Compare Operating Results to Similar Industry Trends
- Liquidation Analysis and Going Concern Value
  - Assess and value collateral
  - Determine perfection of security interests
  - Determine distribution to secured and unsecured
  - Value litigation, notes receivable and noncore assets
- Review NOL Carry-Forwards and Any Cash Flow Benefits

Identify Legal Considerations

- Joint or Separate Plans
- Adequate Protection
- Analysis of Corporate Structure and Assets
- Substantive Consolidation
- Officer and Director Liability and Indemnity
- Classification of Claims by Debtor
- Determination of Amount of Claims of the Debtor
- Preferences, Fraudulent Conveyances and Piercing the Corporate Veil
- Determination of Causes of Action
- Post Petition Operation and Closing Costs, Liabilities and Claims
- Net Operating Losses and Tax Liabilities

Analyze Claims and Priority of Claims

- Identify Debtor's administrative, priority, secured and unsecured claims
- Analyze cash flow from nonbankrupt subsidiaries and beneficiaries to Debtors
- Analyze legal issues such as substantive consolidation

Structure the Plan

- Negotiate Plan with Debtors, Creditors' Groups and Committees
- Items to Consider:
  - Cash payments to certain creditors (ability to pay)
  - Capture increasing value of reorganized company for creditors
    - Debt Instruments:
      - Exchangeable Preferred Stock
      - Common Stock
      - Warrants
  - Equity fix to generate credit and business with contractors
  - Escalating interest and dividend rates
  - Exchange portion of debt for equity
- Mechanics for Sharing in Upside of Business
  - Common stock and warrants
  - Provisions for exchange and/or redemption
  - Contingent cash payments based on operating performance
- Protect Creditors' Positions
  - Restrict new debt and equity issuances to avoid dilution
  - Restrict level of capital expenditures and business expansion
  - Limit secured debt, layering of debt and dividends
  - Board of directors representation
- Management Incentives to Return Business to Optimal Levels
  - Performance-based incentives

Plan Approval Process

- Indenture Trustees and other creditors file proofs of claim on or before bar date as set by the court
- Preparation of the Plan and the Disclosure Statement
- Plan and Disclosure Statements are filed
- Hearing on the adequacy of the Disclosure Statement and approval by the court
- Distribution of the Plan and Disclosure Statement to all creditors who have filed claims
- Approval of the Plan by 2/3 of the amount of claim and 50% of the number of creditors in each class
- If all other Bankruptcy Code requirements are met, then the court will confirm the plan (may "cram down" on junior creditors)
- Upon confirmation, the Debtor is discharged from all pre-petition debts except as provided in the Plan

```
                              ┌─────────────────┐
                              │  Distribution   │
                              └─────────────────┘
```

they need. The analyst should make sure that the company has become lean enough to produce sufficient cash flow to attract a good credit.

Another issue that the analyst must address is taxes. In the early 1980s companies were more willing to take ownership interests in troubled companies because they received the use of the troubled company's net operating loss (NOL) carry-forwards; however, in the mid-1980s, Congress severely restricted their use. If a cancellation of indebtedness (a significant reduction or entire cancellation of debt) occurs outside of bankruptcy, this cancellation is treated as income and can eliminate the NOL. The tax benefit of being able to apply past losses against current or future income is thereby lost. A detailed analysis of NOL treatment and bankruptcy is given in Spiotto (1990). The analyst needs to remember that if debt is reduced without exchanging stock or something else of attributable value, the reduction in debt can become income and thus lead to some loss of the NOL, depending on the tax treatment. The tax attributes of the restructuring cannot be ignored.

Tax problems may be reduced in other ways. For instance, overvalued real estate can be sold at a loss to generate tax losses. In other cases, there are corporate airplanes or headquarters that are of no use to the business itself and can be sold. If you understand the assets and their values, the reorganization process may provide you with additional value.

Legal Considerations

An important part of the reorganization process involves identifying the legal considerations. The analyst must keep in mind that there are many arcane and tedious legal issues involved in a reorganization. **Exhibit 1** lists the major considerations: joint or separate plans; adequate protection; analysis of corporate structure and assets; substantive consolidation; officer and director liability and indemnity; classification of claims by debtor; determination of amount of claims of the debtor; preferences, fraudulent conveyances, and piercing the corporate veil; determination of causes of action; post-petition operation and closing costs, liabilities, and claims; and NOLs and tax liabilities.

Substantive Consolidation. If a holding company and its subsidiaries are in bankruptcy, the company must decide whether it is best to have one big reorganization plan or separate plans for each corporate entity. It makes a difference whether the company is dead at the holding company level or the subsidiary level. If your interests are in the holding company but all the assets are at the subsidiary level—leaving the holding company with too much debt and few assets—you obviously want the prob-

lems treated as a whole. This is known as substantive consolidation.

There are both positive and negative aspects of substantive consolidation. **Table 1** illustrates the benefits. There may be a benefit to the holding company in using substantive consolidation depending on the parent and subsidiary financial condition. Substantive consolidation effectively redistributes the limited resources on a *pro rata* basis by disregarding the claims and their recovery on a separate legal entity basis. Table 1 shows that when the holding company is insolvent but the subsidiaries have net worth, the unsecured creditors may benefit, because recovery is 87 percent with substantive consolidation, compared to only 40 percent without substantive consolidation.

Table 2 illustrates some of the negative aspects of substantive consolidation. For example, there may be an adverse result to the holding company. This table illustrates how the holding company is diluted below its 100 percent recovery on a separate legal entity basis. When the subsidiaries of a holding company are insolvent, but the parent is not, some of the unsecured claims may not be paid in full.

The trend in law has been to move away from substantive consolidation. In the late 1970s and early 1980s, there were some very favorable cases of substantive consolidation in which the entire entity was treated as one because that was the way the subsidiaries operated. The officers were the same and the benefits were passed to the holding company. The subsidiaries were actually more like operating divisions than separate entities.

Automatic Stay. An automatic stay is the immediate barring of all debt collection efforts against the debtor which occurs subsequent to the filing of a voluntary petition under the Bankruptcy Code. The purpose of the Bankruptcy Code is to help people get a fresh start—to protect them from creditors competing to file a lawsuit, get a judgment, and seize property before all the others. The automatic stay is supposed to prevent that situation. A number of years ago, a stay was not automatic; the courts issued one if it was requested. When the Bankruptcy Code was changed in 1978, those things that were previously *de facto* automatic, such as no lawsuits and no protection of security interests, were specifically provided for. Some bankruptcy courts have even interpreted the new code as prohibiting nasty letters to the debtor, although it is difficult to prevent people from doing so. In giving the debtor a fresh start, the idea is to get people to examine the assets carefully.

Liability and Indemnity. Some of the causes of a company's distress, such as suits resulting from securities fraud or environmental issues, can be

Table 1.   Effect of Substantive Consolidation (Benefits)

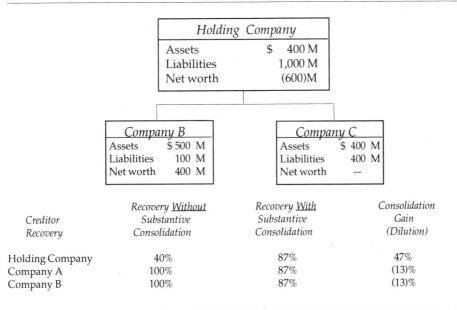

Creditor Recovery	Recovery *Without* Substantive Consolidation	Recovery *With* Substantive Consolidation	Consolidation Gain (Dilution)
Holding Company	40%	87%	47%
Company A	100%	87%	(13)%
Company B	100%	87%	(13)%

tremendously expensive, at least in terms of current cash outlays. Indemnity for officers and directors in these cases is unrealistic. There are ways to deal with this problem, however. In a number of instances, officer and director indemnity claims have been subordinated.

Causes of Action. Many companies that go into bankruptcy may have claims and causes of action. These are claims against officers and directors for mismanagement and fraud, and claims against their insurance carriers. Many companies may have rights to assert these claims but have not done so. It makes sense to look into such litigation, if the facts warrant it, as a possible source of recovery or to provide needed working capital.

Classification of Claims. The classification of claims and the determination of the amount of claims of the debtor is very important. The debtor's claims

Table 2.   Effect of Substantive Consolidation (Detriments)

Holding Company

Assets	$ 5,000 M
Liabilities	5,000 M
Net worth	-0-

Company A

Assets	$ 400 M
Liabilities	1,000 M
Deficit	(500) M

Company B

Assets	$ 2,000 M
Liabilities	1,000 M
Net worth	1,000 M

Company C

Assets	$5,000 M
Liabilities	4,000 M
Net worth	1,000 M

Company D

Assets	$ 2,000 M
Liabilities	4,000 M
Deficit	(2,000)M

Creditor Recovery	Recovery *Without* Substantive Consolidation	Recovery *With* Substantive Consolidation	Consolidation Gain (Dilution)
Holding Company	100%	97%	(3)%
Company A	50%	97%	47%
Company B	100%	97%	(3)%
Company C	100%	97%	(3)%
Company D	50%	97%	47%

and the priority of the claims must be analyzed. **Exhibit 2** illustrates the classification of claims. Administrative claims have the first claim on unencumbered assets (but cannot prime a secured claim), which are paid first. Other claim classifications include the fully secured claims, secured claims, general unsecured claims, convenience classes, senior public debt, bank debt, subordinated debt, and fraud claims and equity interests. Generally, the security fraud claims are subordinated or are below the claim of the security they represent; the purpose of this is to prevent someone who has sold the security to be ahead of someone who still has the contractual right to be paid on the note or debenture.

Exhibit 3 shows how different classes of claims are paid under the absolute priority rule. If you hold senior debt, you need to watch for secured and administrative claims. If you hold subordinated debt, you want to be sure that not only are the claims above you classified, but that they are classified down to the lowest level possible. If you hold debt, you should be alert to any excess claims or claims that can be equitably subordinated, such as claims of officers and directors, related companies, or entities that should be below you for equity reasons.

Fraudulent Conveyances. Another important area to consider is fraudulent conveyances, which are attempts to hinder, delay, and deceive one's creditors by transferring assets to another entity. In simple terms, this practice can be illustrated as follows: There were two brothers; one brother had a cow—but also lots of creditors—so he gave the cow to his brother; as a result, even though his creditors could get him thrown in jail, they couldn't get anything else. This issue has become far more complicated in today's environment, where cases are concerned with billions of dollars rather than one cow.

There is a great debate today about whether leveraged buyouts (LBOs) are fraudulent conveyances. One problem is that the legal definition of an

Exhibit 2.   Classification of Claims

Class	Type of Claim	Possible Treatment
Class 1	Administrative Claim (Priority and Tax claims may be classified separately)	Must be paid in full upon confirmation (Tax claims within six years of assessment)
Class 2	Fully Secured Claims (if any)	Payment in full or cure all defaults and provide assurance of future performance
Class 3	Secured Claims (which have collateral value less than debt outstanding)	Secured Claim for value of collateral with market rate terms
Class 4	General Unsecured Claims (Trade Debt and deficiency claim on Class 3 unsecured portion)	Cash, Notes, or Equity or a combination of all
Class 5	Convenience Class of General Unsecured Claims, for example $10,000 or less (or claims above $10,000 that reduce claim to $10,000)	Set recovery of a fixed amount of cents on the dollar
Class 6	Senior Public Debt	Cash, Notes, or Equity (same as Class 4) plus the benefits of subordination
Class 7	Banks and money borrowed: creditor entitled to benefits of subordination (could be Class 3 deficiency claim)	Cash, Notes, or Equity (same as Class 4) plus the benefits of subordination
Class 8	Public Subordinated Debt	Cash, Notes, or Equity (same as Class 4) minus payment on subordination to the degree it is effective
Class 9	Security Fraud Claims of Class 7	Depends on amounts of Cash, Notes, and Equity available after satisfying lower numbered classes
Class 10	Security Fraud Claims of Class 8	Depends on amounts of Cash, Notes, and Equity available after satisfying lower numbered classes
Class 11	Equity Interests	Depends on equity available after satisfying lower numbered classes

Exhibit 3.   Absolute Priority: Schematic of Payment (Debt/Equity)

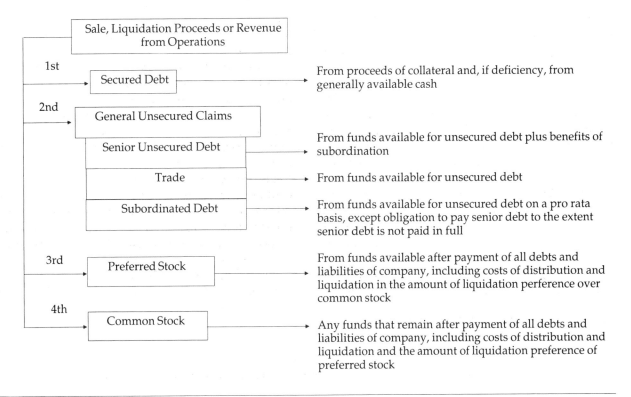

LBO is not the same for all jurisdictions, so there are some areas where LBOs are considered fraudulent conveyances and other areas where they are not.

If you extend credit at the time of an LBO, knowing the details of the transaction, it is difficult to argue later that you were the victim of a fraudulent conveyance. If you are an older creditor who had "relied on the cow" when extending credit, then the conveyance should not work.

Analysis of Claims and Priority of Claims

Once the company's financial condition has been analyzed and the legal considerations have been identified, the claims and priority of claims must be analyzed. This involves three steps: (1) identify the debtor's administrative, priority, secured, and unsecured claims; (2) analyze the cash flow from non-bankrupt subsidiaries and the beneficiaries to debtors; and (3) analyze the legal issues, such as substantive consolidation.

The methodology for analyzing claims and the priority of claims is illustrated in **Exhibit 4**. The process involves asking a series of questions: Is the claim secured? Is it unsecured? Does it have other rights? Is it equity? An equity claim receives special treatment because it is not paid or treated until after all the other creditors get paid in full.

Compare your claim to the other claims. If the claim is secured, examine the security first. If it is unsecured, then it receives what the general unsecured creditors do. If it is subordinated, the question is whether the subordination is effective. Only in rare cases is the subordinated debt totally wiped out. Theoretically, subordinated debt is paid out of funds available for general unsecured claims, but it yields to senior unsecured debt, if that class is not paid in full.

The absolute priority rule, illustrated in Exhibit 3, states that payments to any class (first, second, third, fourth) can only be made once the class(es) above it have been paid in full. To form a consensual plan in bankruptcy, the general unsecured creditors will often allow a small amount to be paid to preferred and common stock in order to avoid further objections, delays, and controversy.

Exhibit 5 shows the distribution of cash and the claim analysis. It starts with the total amount of the claims and then moves to some reduction resulting from disallowed disputed claims. Normally, some of the claimants will have calculated interest payments incorrectly, they will have owed the debtor some money, or a similar situation will exist. So

Exhibit 4.   Methodology for Analyzing Claims and the Priority of Claims

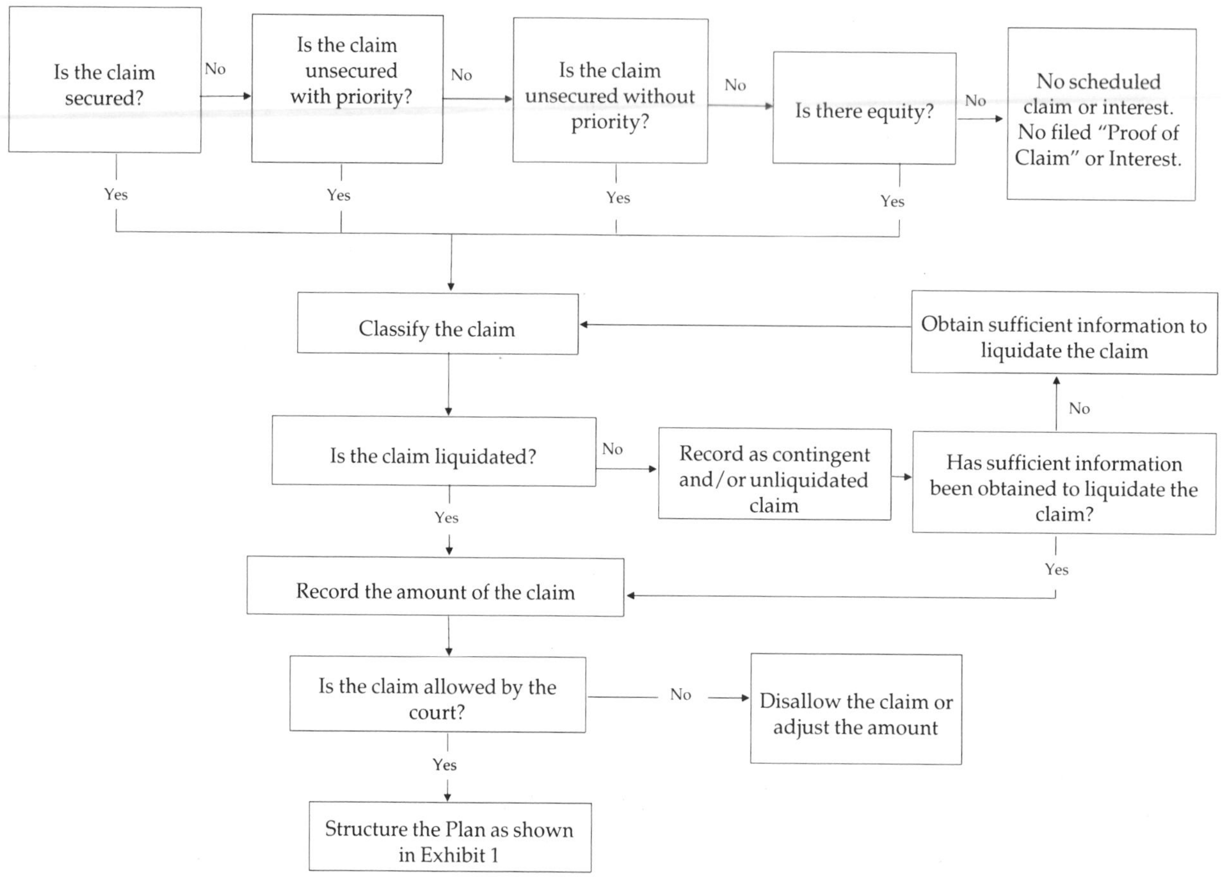

these claims are reduced or eliminated to arrive at an allowed claims figure. Then the flow is similar to that discussed above.

Structuring the Plan

After analyzing the company's financial condition, identifying the relevant legal considerations, and analyzing the claims and priorities, the next step is to structure the plan. This involves negotiating with debtors, creditors' groups, and committees. Dealing with creditors in drawing up a reorganization plan can involve a lot of creativity and offer tremendous opportunities. Many companies are destroyed at this stage by intransigence or by simply tiring of thinking of new alternatives.

The financial analyst is in a position to analyze the credits and reshuffle them so that these companies can be made to work. People involved with bankruptcies, especially the creditors' committees, sometimes lack the financial acumen and insight to properly structure a credit going forward. Everything must be examined: the types of securities available, the income available to service them, whether the

service should be cash pay or payment in kind, the type of interest payments, and the possibilities for upside potential with warrants, stock, or put rights. It is also important to keep management in mind: The plan should include incentives to ensure that management personnel cooperate and remain motivated.

The debenture indentures should contain enough covenants at the onset, as they did in the late 1960s and early 1970s. In the latter part of the 1970s and in the 1980s, too little was put into indentures— there were too few covenants and, in some cases, they were not properly worded. Today we recognize the problems that this caused, so the trend is back to more covenants.

The Plan Approval Process

Once the plan has been structured, it must be approved. This involves building a consensus. Because the trade creditors usually want to be on the creditors' committee, now the trend is to have separate bondholder and noteholder committees. This is something that rarely existed in the 1970s.

Exhibit 5. Allocation of Cash to Classes of Claims Based on Priorities and Funds Availability after the Plan Effective Date

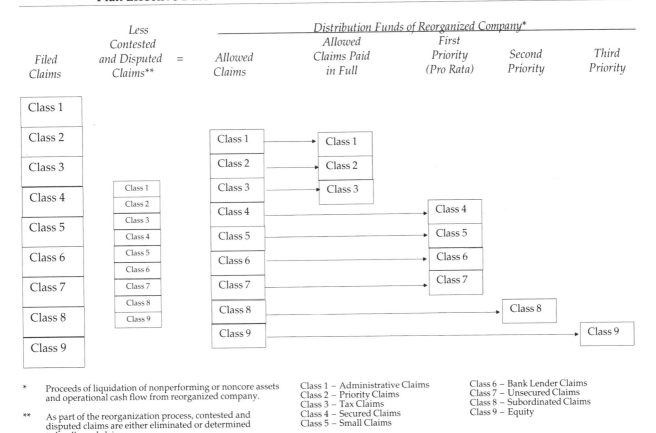

* Proceeds of liquidation of nonperforming or noncore assets and operational cash flow from reorganized company.

** As part of the reorganization process, contested and disputed claims are either eliminated or determined to be allowed claims.

Class 1 – Administrative Claims
Class 2 – Priority Claims
Class 3 – Tax Claims
Class 4 – Secured Claims
Class 5 – Small Claims

Class 6 – Bank Lender Claims
Class 7 – Unsecured Claims
Class 8 – Subordinated Claims
Class 9 – Equity

It is important to work with the indenture trustee on public debt to make sure that there is an analysis of all the facts that you, as a reasonable investor, ought to know. Bankruptcy judges and lawyers sometimes do not know what is significant to investors, so your insight and ability are important in determining the content of the disclosure statement, which is akin to the prospectus on the reorganization.

In building the consensus to get the plan approved, it is necessary to receive the approval of at least one class, which involves getting the votes of two-thirds of the dollar amount and 50 percent of the number of the class. For example, if the claims on a class amount to $100 million, at least $66.66 million and one-half of the number of the claims must vote for the plan.

Participants in the reorganization process must ensure that they get the deal that they want. Often, there is pressure to relinquish claims and causes of action against such third parties as officers and directors. Participants should be aware that these claims do not need to be given up in bankruptcy.

Distribution

The final step in the reorganization is distribution pursuant to the terms of the plan or reorganization.

The Restructuring Process

The restructuring process is similar to the reorganization process. The principal thing that distinguishes a restructuring from a bankruptcy is the fact that the restructuring occurs outside of a court. There is no judge to turn to when disagreements arise or someone wishes to assert a claim or cause of action. In a restructuring, everyone must go along with the plan, so persuasion is often necessary. In bankruptcy, on the other hand, with only 66 ⅔ of the dollar amount and one class of creditors required to accept the plan, the bankruptcy court can find the plan to be fair and equitable, thus, for all practical purposes, forcing it on the other creditors. **Exhibit 6**

Exhibit 6. Overview of the Restructuring Process

Restructuring Proposed by the Company

↓

Ascertain the Company's Assets and Liabilities

- Assess the Company's Capital Structure
  - Equity Securities
  - Debt Securities–Including Subordination Provisions and Collateral Position
  - Bank Debt, Other Debt and Liabilities–(Including long term contracts, purchase money obligations, leases, employment obligations, indemnity or contribution, lawsuits, deferred taxes, costs of restructuring)
- Identify and value assets–(Including net operating loss carry-forwards, causes of action, and intellectual property)

↓

Analyze the Company's Business and Operations

- Understand the Company's Business
- Compare the Company's Competitive Position in its Industry Segments
- Request that the Company's Management Prepare a Business Plan
  - (Including profit improvement programs, revenue enhancers, new product lines, summaries of historical data and trends, capital expenditures, overhead and expense allocations, inventory controls, and management)

↓

Assess the Company's Financial Condition

- Request that the Company Prepare Financial Projections
  - (Include the following: historical data, projected cash flows and income statements, capital expenditure budget, and analyses of data)
- Review Projections
- Compare Operating Results to Similar Industry Trends
- Liquidation Analysis and Going Concern Value
  - Including determining security interest perfection and valuing litigation, notes receivable and noncore assets
- Review Net Operating Loss Carry-Forwards and Any Cash Flow Benefits
- Stop the Bleeding
  - Identify losing operations, poor-performing personnel and divisions
  - Develop plan (sell cash users, enhance operations of cash producers, right size personnel)

↓

Negotiate the Terms of the Restructuring Plan
Prepare Counter-Proposal to the Company's Restructuring Plan

- Negotiate Restructuring Plan with Creditors and Company/Prepare Counter-Proposal to the Company's Plan
- Items to Consider:
  - Capture increasing value of restructured company for creditors
    - Using Senior Notes, Subordinated Debentures, Exchangeable Preferred Stock, Convertible Preferred Stock, Common Stock, or Warrants
  - Escalating interest and dividend rates
  - Exchange portion of debt for equity
  - Share in Upside of Business
    - Using common stock, warrants, provisions for exchange and/or redemption or contingent cash payments
- Protect Creditors' Positions
  - Restrict new debt and equity issuances to avoid dilution
  - Restrict the level of capital expenditures and business expansion
  - Limit secured debt, layering of debt and dividends
  - Board of director representation
- Encourage Management to Return Business to Optimal Levels
- Share the Pain Equally Among Creditor Groups

↓

Restructuring Plan Approval Process

- The Company's Board of Directors approves the Restructuring Plan
- The Company may file a Registration Statement Prospectus with the Securities and Exchange Commission (SEC) reflecting the terms of the Restructuring Plan or comply with exemption. Obtain approval of the SEC or alternatively obtain court approval of workout with notice to all affected creditors. The documents may be amended from time to time.
- The Company sends a solicitation package to the creditors, containing any necessary consents and guaranteed delivery contracts.
- Consents received must reach the predetermined threshold level (usually 90-95%) or obtain binding court order.
- If the number of consents is sufficient, or an effective binding court order, the security holders may tender their securities and receive new securities.
- If the number of consents is not sufficient, the Company may choose to extend the period for solicitation, lower the threshold level, or file bankruptcy.

↓

Implement Restructuring Plan

provides an overview of the restructuring process.

The analysis of the plan is the same for both processes. Cash flow must be examined, a debt structure must be designed, and the company's financial condition must be assessed in order to maximize recovery. It is extremely important to know about all the claims, if possible, when the situation is handled outside of the bankruptcy court. In an outside debt restructuring, if the public debt is the only problem treated, there could be environmental liabilities, labor problems, pension fund liabilities, or off-balance-sheet problems that will not be included. The debt restructuring could explode in your face when those issues emerge.

An outside debt restructuring should be negotiated in the same way that a plan of reorganization is: try to build a consensus and to get everyone to go along. If this is not possible, a way out is to get a prepackaged plan, which involves getting the creditors to sign an acceptance and ballot for a plan of reorganization prior to the bankruptcy filing. This counts and is binding. If the disclosure is sufficient as required by the Bankruptcy Code, and two-thirds by face value and 50 percent by number of the class approve, the bankruptcy court can confirm the plan. Then the worry is about meeting the absolute priority rule or exceeding it by giving something to lower-tranche creditors.

The debt restructuring process is where questions should be asked, cash flow understood, problems sorted out, and a workable plan formulated. Much money can be saved by doing this outside of bankruptcy in the form of a prepackaged plan. One other way of doing it is what is known as a Section 3(a)(10) proceeding. Under some circumstances this can be the fastest way of doing a debt restructuring. It involves filing an action against the obligor and making it a class action binding on the entire class of debtholders. If a reasonable and fair settlement can be reached, the court can approve it. This grants the new debt an exemption from registration under Section 3(a)(10) of the Securities Act of 1933.

Conclusion

Unfortunately, financial analysts are finding it necessary to understand the bankruptcy and workout process. While each situation is unique, the basic principles should govern your assessment of a credit both prior to and after default. The next several years will reveal more clearly the successes and failures in the reorganization and restructuring process.

Question and Answer Session

Question: Do tax claims come before or after the claims of secured debt?

Spiotto: The type of tax claim determines its ranking. For instance, with a real estate tax claim, the claim is against the property. To sell the property, the tax claim will have to be settled first, so this type of claim would precede secured debt. With something like a pension liability claim, the claim is not connected to any property per se, and it does not have statutory priority above the mortgage. Therefore, those claims would not come ahead of the secured lender. Likewise, any income tax claims owed to the IRS would not be ahead of a secured claim, unless the IRS put a lien on the property prior to the time that the secured creditors perfected their security interests.

Question: Where does ESOP debt and equity fall in priority of claims, and does it make any difference if the ESOP is established as a pension plan?

Spiotto: There have not been any real tests of ESOP priority over the past few years. Generally, the ESOP notes should be treated as debt to the degree that they are labelled as debt. There may be a problem, however, if the ESOP has a degree of equity interest. In cases as far back as the 1950s, when someone owns both debt and equity, or has control of the company, their debt and equity become subordinated to the general unsecured creditors. To the extent that a creditor has a controlling equity interest, he runs the risk of having the equity interest declared as his prevailing interest and having his notes and loans subordinated. In effect, the debt becomes a capital contribution. To avoid this, the plan must be structured properly, classifying notes and loans as such.

Question: Does the risk of having an LBO declared a fraudulent conveyance cause extra emphasis to be placed on the fair market value opinion that is obtained at the time of the LBO?

Spiotto: People take those opinions very seriously, often to the chagrin of those who gave the opinion. The parties participating in an LBO can lock in the values of their positions. For example, for a solvent company, if the transaction is a contemporaneous, fair, and equivalent exchange of value, there may not even be an LBO. To the degree that the money is kept in the company, there is no fraudulent conveyance. It is only when money goes out to the shareholders that these problems arise.

You should expect to see the certification and opinions getting tighter in the future. There will also be a trend toward keeping money in the company or limiting the amount passed to the shareholders so that the secured creditors do not feel that their value has diminished. An example might be the issuance of new subordinated debt with the proceeds from that going out to the shareholders, thus keeping the secured debt value in the company.

Question: Is there a major difference between an insolvency of an industrial enterprise and an insolvency of a bank or other financial institution?

Spiotto: With a regular industrial corporation bankruptcy, everything is open and above board in court. When dealing with a financial institution, however, you often will not hear anything from the regulators for long periods of time, only to find out some weekend that the institution has been closed. Dealing with a financial institution, whether it is through the FDIC or the Resolution Trust Corp, is a different world from dealing with an industrial enterprise. People that have been involved with troubled financial firms often claim that they have trouble negotiating with the government and cannot get any answers.

Question: If there is a change in stock ownership exceeding 50 percent in a bankruptcy, is there some way that the creditors can block that change in ownership to preserve the NOL?

Spiotto: Yes, given several restrictions. The present equity must be held in a voting trust for 36 months, which is the period of time for which change of ownership is measured. Then there may be either new debt, additional debt, or equity going to the creditors. Voting trusts can be used to hold equity as long as the ownership right to vote the security does not change. When the voting trust is set up, the board of directors is determined for the next three years. The old equity has voting power, but it cannot change the reorganization plan. After the three years have passed, the equity can then be distributed from the voting trust.

Estimating Cash Flows

James A. Gentry
IBE Distinguished Professor of Finance
University of Illinois

In the 1970s, I became convinced that the concept of cash flow was not clearly understood. A book by Eric Helfert (1982), which contains a full presentation of cash flow, was a motivating influence to pursue the topic in greater depth. Over time, the idea developed that bankruptcy might be predicted by using some type of cash flow analysis. That idea has been extended into predicting bond ratings and bank loan risk ratings. In this presentation, I will develop the idea of free cash flow and how it can be used to explain bankruptcy. I will discuss how the components of cash flow can be used to predict financial distress or failure.

Cash Flow Components

Free cash flow is defined as the net cash flow available after taking into account all cash inflows and outflows. **Exhibit 1** presents the components of free cash flow with an example of the free cash flow calculation. This framework shows the source of the cash inflows and where the cash outflows are being used. It is instructive to look at both absolute and relative cash flow components.

Exhibit 1 illustrates the following steps involved in calculating the cash flow components:

1. Calculate the *net operating cash flow*, which is the difference between sales and operating expenses (in the example, this is $1,200).
2. Calculate the *net investment cash flow*, which is the sum of change in net fixed assets plus depreciation expenses. In the example, this is $720. Free cash flow after investment is equal to the net operating cash flow minus the net investment cash flow, $1,200 – $720 = $480.
3. Determine *discretionary cash flows*—the dividends and fixed coverage expenditures (interest plus leasing expenses). Free cash flow before working capital is equal to free cash flow after investment less dividends and fixed coverage expenditures. In the example, free cash flow before working capital is $100.
4. Calculate the *net working capital cash flows*. In many businesses, changes in working capital constitute a major use of cash. Typically, banks pay a lot of attention to the net working capital position. Using the numbers given in Exhibit 1, the three current asset classes used $860 in cash: the increase in accounts receivable is $440, the increase in inventories is $360, and the increase in other current assets is $60. The increase in accounts payable and other current liabilities only contributed $300 to offset the cash outflow for current assets. The change in working capital equals ($560); [($860) – $300 = ($560)].

   Changes in the working capital position are added to the free cash flow before working capital figure to determine free cash flow after changes in working capital of ($460); [($560) + $100 = ($460)]. This means the remaining net operating cash flow has been consumed by the change in working capital, plus an additional $460. It is important to note that at this point all of the major cash flows have been taken into account.
5. Calculate the *financial cash flows*, which are the cash flows arising from selling long- and short-term debt, and from selling common or preferred stock. There are $340 of financing cash inflows. After receiving the financing cash flows, the company is only short $120 instead of $460. Additionally, changes in the other assets and other liabilities accounts contributed to the net cash outflow.

Thus, the total net cash outflow is $160, which was offset by a $160 reduction in the cash and marketable securities accounts. The nice thing about a cash flow analysis is that total inflows equal total outflows, so the free cash flow after accounting for all the components equals zero.

From the viewpoint of management, free cash flow is the amount of cash flow that remains after changes in working capital. From the point of view of the analyst, constructing free cash flow measures illustrates where the cash comes from and how it is spent. The analyst should be interested in the sustainability of the free cash flow after working capital and whether it can be used as a basis for explaining

Exhibit 1. Cash Flow Measurement

Type of Cash Flow	Inputs	Example
Operating		
Inflows	Sales	$2,000
Outflows	Cost of sales + SGA expenses + Taxes (500 + 100 + 200)	(800)
Net operating cash flow (NOCF)		$1,200
Investment		
Inflow	Decrease in net fixed assets (NFA)	$ 0
Outflow	Increase in NFA + Depreciation expense (400 + 320)	$ (720)
Net investment cash flow (NICF)		
Free cash flow after investment	= NOCF − NICF	$ 480
Dividend (DIV)		$ (200)
Fixed coverage expenditures (FCE)	Interest paid + leasing expense	$ (180)
Free cash flow before working capital	= NOCF − NICF − DIV − FCE	$ 100
Working capital	Inflow(+) Outflow(−)	
Δ Accounts receivable (AR)	Δ AR↓ Δ AR↑	(440)
Δ Inventory (INV)	Δ INV↓ Δ INV↑	(360)
Δ Other current assets (OCA)	Δ OCA Δ OCA↑	(60)
Δ Accounts payable (AP)	Δ AP↑ Δ AP↓	200
Δ Other current liabilities (OCL)	Δ OCL↑ Δ OCL↓	100
Change in working capital		(560)
Free cash flow after change in working capital	= NOCF − NICF − DIV − FCE − Δ AR −Δ INV − Δ OCA − Δ AR − ΔOCL	$ (460)
Financial		
Inflows	Δ LTD↑ + Δ STB↑ + Δ CS↑	$ 340
Outflows	Δ LTD↓ + Δ STB↓ + Δ CS↓	—
Net financial (NFCF)		$ 340
Other Assets and Liabilities		
Inflows	Δ OA↓ + Δ OL↑	$
− Outflows	Δ OA↑ + Δ OL↓	(40)
= Net Other A&L	NOAL	(40)
Free Cash Flow After Eleven Cash Flows		(160)
Change in Cash (ΔC)	= (Ending Cash + Marketable Securities) − (Beginning Cash + Marketable Securities)	160
Free Cash Flow After All Flows		0

Note: ( ) indicates cash outflow.

Source: James A. Gentry

the causes of bankruptcy.

The power of a cash flow analysis is illustrated in **Exhibit 2**, which is a reconciliation of income and cash flow. The first column summarizes the components of net income as presented in an income statement. After subtracting all the costs from the sales, the net income turns out to be $700, and retained earnings increase by $500. The next two columns show the adjustments needed to reconcile earnings with cash flow. Take, for example, the reconciliation of cash received from the sale of products. The company sold $2,000 worth of the product, but did not receive $2,000 in cash. The revenue must be adjusted for changes in accounts receivable, in this case an increase of $400, resulting in $1,560 of cash generated from sales. The other adjustments are made in a similar way.

The actual net cash flow ends up being $40 ver-

sus net income of $700. After paying dividends of $200, the resulting net cash flow shortfall is $160, which is exactly what was obtained in Exhibit 1 as the decrease in the cash account.

Interpreting Financial Performance

The cash flow analysis can be used to identity distressed and bankrupt firms versus healthy firms. The first step in such an analysis is to calculate the relative cash flows. **Exhibit 3** summarizes the absolute cash flow components used in Exhibit 1. These data are categorized into inflows and outflows. From the absolute cash flow values the relative cash flows may be calculated. That is, each inflow component is divided by the total cash inflows, and the same for the outflow components.

In this example, 60 percent of the cash inflow comes from net operating cash flows and approximately 17 percent from net financing cash flows. On the outflow side, net investment accounts for 36 percent of the total outflow and receivables account for 22 percent.

Once the cash flow components are calculated on a relative basis, it is possible to compare companies. **Table 1** shows an example of the hierarchy of relative cash flow components and relative free cash flow measures under various risk conditions. For example, compare the lowest-risk company category to the highest-risk company category. The company that has 100 percent of its cash inflow coming from operations is in the lowest risk category. It has few restrictions; it does not have to borrow; it does not

have to use its existing cash to offset shortfalls; and it can add any free cash to its cash and marketable securities portfolio. So the company with very high operating cash flows has substantive financial strengths. In the highest risk category, the company has only 25 percent of its cash inflows coming from net operating cash flows.

Firms that are spending between 35 and 50 percent of the total outflow on investment, depending on the industry, tend to be the fairly strong companies. That means that the relative free cash flow after investment is going to be about 60 percent. It has also been observed that, for fairly strong firms, approximately 10 percent of the total outflow goes toward dividends.

Firms that are financially strong may have some

Exhibit 2. Reconciliation of Earnings and Cash Flow

	Earnings	Source (Inflow)	Use (Outflow)	Cash Flow
		Adjustments		
Sales	$2,000			
Δ Receivables			$440	
Net cash flow				$1,560
Cost of Sales	$500			
Δ Inventory			$360	
Δ Payables		$200		
Δ Other current assets			$60	
Δ Other current liabilities		$100		
Net cash outflow				($620)
SG&A expenses	$100			
Net other A&L			$40	
Net cash outflow				($140)
Depreciation expense	$320			
Δ Net fixed assets			$400	
Net cash outflow				($720)
EBIT	$1,080			
Fixed coverage expense	$180			
Δ Short-term debt				
Δ Long-term debt		$340		
Δ Preferred				
Δ Common stock				
Net cash outflow				$160
Earnings before taxes	$900			
Income tax expense	$200			
Δ Deferred taxes				
Net cash flow				($200)
Net cash flow				$40
Net income	$700			
–Dividends	$200			($200)
Retained earnings	$500			
Net cash flow after dividends				($160)
Note: ( ) indicates a cash outflow.				

Source: James A. Gentry

debt outstanding, but it is generally quite small, so only a small proportion of the total outflow goes to interest payments. Such a company would have a high coverage ratio.

For the lowest risk category, a company might spend 10 percent of its cash inflow on dividends and 5 percent on net fixed coverage expenditures. Thus, Company A in Table 1 has free cash flow before working capital of 45 percent. If the change in net working capital equals 10 percent of net cash inflows, the free cash flow after working capital is 35 percent. This means that, if the company started with 100 percent of cash inflow from operating sources, they still have around 35 percent left that can be used to retire debt or common stock, or build up the cash account. This describes the strongest kind of company, e.g., Eli Lilly and R.R. Donnelly.

This hierarchy turns out to be important in determining financial strengths or weaknesses. Our research has shown that the high-risk companies have relatively low net operating cash flow, net investment, and dividends, but high fixed coverage expenditures. They also look like companies that have failed in the past.

The numbers shown in Table 1 for the cash flow hierarchy do, of course, vary substantially among industries. The hierarchy example demonstrates the differences that exist between risk classes. Table 1 shows as total risk increases, net operating cash inflow becomes a smaller proportion of the total, and net investment declines as a percent of the total outflow. The example indicates that for the highest-risk firms, there is very little free cash flow remaining after investment. Distressed firms and firms approaching failure usually do not pay dividends, but interest payments typically comprise 15 percent of the total cash outflow for these firms. In the hierarchy presented, this means that there is no free cash flow available to meet working capital needs. Not only have the net operating cash flows been consumed, but an additional 25 percent has also been spent.

For riskier firms, the free cash flow after working capital becomes quite negative. Because these firms must get additional money from somewhere, there will have to be a substantial inflow from financing, for example 50 to 75 percent of the total inflows, unless the firm still has cash. It also often happens that the net other assets and liabilities, which are accrued accounts, decline.

In a 1985 study, I compared the relative cash flow components of a sample of 33 firms that failed with

Exhibit 3.   Summary of Cash Flows

Absolute Cash Flow Components

Inflows		Outflows	
Net operating	$1,200	Δ Receivables	$440
Δ Payables	200	Δ Inventory	360
Δ Other current liabilities	100	Δ Other cash assets	60
Δ Net financial	340	Δ Fixed coverage expenses	180
Δ Cash M.S.	60	Δ Net investment	720
		Dividends	200
		Net other A&L	40
Total	$2,000	Total	$2,000

Relative Cash Flow Components

	% of Total Net Cash flow		% of Total Net Cash flow
Net operating*	60	Δ Receivables*	22
Δ Payables*	10	Δ Inventory*	18
Δ Other current liabilities*	5	Δ Other current assets*	3
Δ Net financing*	17	Fixed coverage expenses*	9
Δ Cash M.S.*	8	Net investment*	36
		Dividends*	10
		Δ Net other A&L*	2
Total	100%	Total	100%

Note:

$$\frac{\text{Absolute cash flow components}}{\text{Total net cash flow}} = \text{Relative cash flow components}$$

*Indicates relative as opposed to absolute cash flow.

Source: James A. Gentry

Table 1. An Example of the Hierarchy of Relative Cash Flow Components and Relative Free Cash Flow (FCF*) Measures under Various Risk Conditions

| | Company | | | |
| | Lowest Risk | | Highest Risk | |
Relative Cash Flow Measures	A	B	C	D
Net operating cash flows	100%	75%	50%	25%
Net investment cash flows	−40	−35	−30	−20
Free cash flow (FCF) after investment	60	40	20	5
Dividends*	−10	−15	−20	0
Fixed Coverage Expenses (FCE*)	− 5	−10	−15	−30
FCF* Before Working Capital	45	15	−15	−25
Δ Net Working Capital (Δ NWC*)[1]	−10	− 8	−5	0
FCF* After Working Capital	35%	7%	−20%	−25%
Δ Net Financing				75
Δ Net Other A&L				−50
Δ Cash and Marketable Securities				−50

[1] Δ NWC* = Δ ARF* + Δ INVF* + Δ OCA* + Δ AP* + Δ OCL*

*Indicates relative as opposed to absolute cash flow.

Source: Loque, D.E., ed. 1990. *Handbook of Modern Finance*, Second Edition. Boston: Warren, Gorham & Lamont.

a sample of firms that did not fail to determine which cash flow components were good discriminators between the groups.[1] The most significant cash flow variable in discriminating between failed and non-failed companies is dividends. The next most important variables are cash outflows going to capital investment and accounts receivable. The firms that did not fail spent on average 39 percent of their total outflow on investment expenditures, while for failed companies, the mean outflow for capital expenditures was 16 percent. Dividends accounted for 9 percent of outflows for companies that do not fail, whereas most companies that failed had not been paying dividends.

The results also show that neither the net operating cash flow nor the fixed charge coverage ratio was important in predicting failure. The results indicate that the mean operating cash inflow of companies that did not fail was 56 percent, and 26 percent for the failed companies. There was a high variance for the failed companies, which probably explains why they are not a good discriminator. Some bankrupt companies are still doing very well operationally before they fail, although the operations of others are doing poorly. For companies that did not fail, the mean fixed charge coverage ratio was around 8 per-

cent, but for failed companies the mean ratio was 15 percent or higher.

Another variable that turned out to be important was accounts receivable. In firms that did not fail, accounts receivable, on average, were used to expand the business. For firms that failed, the mean change in accounts receivable was an inflow of cash. This is not surprising. Firms that are close to failing try to collect cash as rapidly as possible, reducing the accounts receivable. Furthermore, as sales decline, the accounts receivable decline.

So the three variables that turned out to be the most important in this study were dividends, investment, and accounts receivable. The two that many people consider most important, operating cash flow and fixed coverage expenses, were not statistically significant.

Stability of Free Cash Flow Characteristics

The stability of a company's cash flow components is important because it is closely related to the risk rating assigned by a rating agency. The information from Table 1 is used to develop graphics that illustrate the relationship between relative free cash flow after working capital (FCF*) and financial risk

---

[1] Gentry, Newbold, and Whitford (1985a, 1985b).

measures.

Figure 1 illustrates the pattern of relative free cash flows after working capital for different risk categories. It shows that companies with high relative free cash flow are classified as having the lowest risk, e.g., Company A in Table 1. As the FCF* declines the financial risk of a company increases. For example, when the FCF* is approximately zero, the company would be classified as having average financial risk. When the FCF* is negative, the financial risk increases, as evidenced in Companies C and D in Table 1.

Figure 2 illustrates another way of presenting the relative risk of a company based on the free cash flow analysis. A time series of FCF* shows what is happening both strategically and operationally within a company in a 10-year period. A company with consistently high FCF* and low variability will be classified as being a low-risk firm. This type of company would be located in the upper part of Figure 2. A company with a 20-percent FCF* might receive an above-average rating. The average firm probably uses up most of its operating flows to cover investment, dividends, fixed charges, and working capital. The company with an average risk class would have mean zero FCF* over time and be located in the middle of Figure 2. As the free cash flow becomes negative and the variability increases, firms are classified as having high financial risk and are located at the bottom of Figure 2. These are the firms that have the potential to be financially distressed.

Figure 3 synthesizes the variability of the rela-

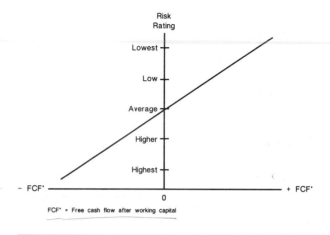

Figure 1.   Risk Rating and Free Cash Flow

FCF* = Free cash flow after working capital

Source: James A. Gentry

tive free cash flow and its association with the risk classes. For the highest-rated firms, FCF* has modest variability. These firms, with the lowest risk ratings, would be located in the upper left area of Figure 3. The free cash flow of companies that are doing poorly tend to have substantial variability. These would be the distressed companies and they would be plotted in the lower right section of Figure 3. A worst-case scenario would be a company that never had a positive free cash flow after working capital.

We recently performed an analysis that used the S&P stock ratings as measures of risk for 24 pharmaceutical companies and 24 food companies. Com-

Figure 2.   Time Series Patterns of Free Cash Flow and Risk Class

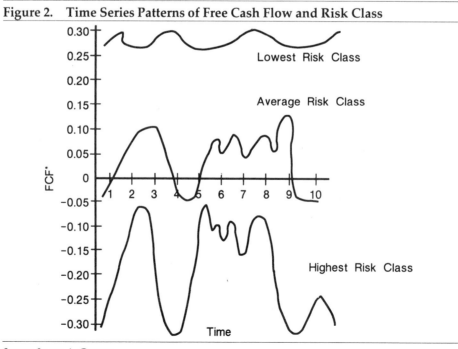

Source: James A. Gentry

Figure 3. Variability of Free Cash Flow and Risk Class

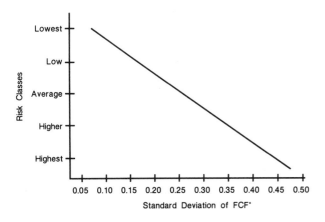

Source: James A. Gentry

panies that had a high standardization of free cash flow for the period 1980-89 were assigned a high risk rating, while a low risk rating was assigned to firms with low standard deviation. The R^2 for both samples was 0.64.

Conclusion

Relative free cash flow after all major expenditures (FCF*) provides an insightful and intuitively appealing measure of corporate performance. There is a significant relationship between assigned risk ratings and the variability of FCF*. That is, the higher the standard deviation of FCF*, the greater the financial risk of a company. Companies that experience negative FCF* for a prolonged period are also in the high-risk class. Thus, companies that have high variability of negative FCF* are more than likely experiencing financial distress. Analyzing the contributions of the major cash flow components supplies unique historical insights into the operating and strategic performance of a company. Determining the ability of a company to significantly improve its FCF* is at the heart of the investment decision involving a distressed company.

Question and Answer Session

Question: How do you deal with non-cash interest expenditures (for example, payment-in-kind securities) in your cash flow analysis?

Gentry: We have not examined non-cash interest expenditures explicitly. But I can make an observation on how the cash flow will be incorporated after the fact. These expenditures will create a very high financing outflow, maybe 50 or 60 percent of the total outflow, at the end of the time period, which is when most of them come due.

Question: Clearly, the investment component is one of the critical factors. By reducing investment, companies undermine the viability of an enterprise. But have you accounted for the prospective sales of property, plant, and equipment, and divisions in an LBO?

Gentry: By selling off large quantities of fixed assets after the transaction, investment would become a positive number and thus be an inflow. Our study was done in 1982, which was before LBOs became so popular. If the study were to be repeated now, however, the investment variable would most likely behave differently, probably with more variability and less significance.

Question: What data sources did you use in your study? Were there problems of lack of comparability in the composition of the companies and the characteristics of reporting?

Gentry: All the companies came from the Compustat tapes. We used both the regular tape as well as the special tape that contains information on failed companies. So all the companies in the study have been traded on an exchange. The initial sample contained 105 failed companies for the period from 1970 to 1982. Because we needed at least five years of complete balance sheet and income statement data, the resulting sample contained only 33 companies. We matched those firms with 33 other companies, in the same industry and of approximately the same size, that did not fail.

Question: What is the best source for gaining an understanding of the cash flow accounting process?

Gentry: I think that Eric Helfert's *Techniques in Financial Analysis* is the best. He does not break down the cash flow components the way I have, but the ideas are very well developed.

Question: How much variability is there in the percentages-per-cash-flow component within a risk class and between industries?

Gentry: There is a high degree of stability in strong, dominant companies, but the instability increases dramatically as you move toward marginal companies and companies with problems. From the two examples that I have, the standard deviation for high-risk companies is sometimes two to four times greater than the mean free cash flow. For relatively low-risk companies, the standard deviation may only be half as large as the mean. So, the mean cash flow would be substantially larger than the variance.

Question: Why are taxes grouped with operating expenditures, when they are greatly influenced by property additions, depreciation, and all those other non-operating factors?

Gentry: The relation between taxes and operations was developed by Helfert. My only justification for including them there is that he felt that taxes were important when considering operating flows.

Using Cash Flows and Financial Ratios to Predict Bankruptcies

Frank K. Reilly, CFA
Bernard J. Hank Professor of Business Administration
University of Notre Dame

There has been a significant increase in bankruptcies and defaults on bonds in recent years. Although the default rates for 1990 are not known, the final results will probably not be very encouraging. Given the number of high-yield bonds issued, there will be many more bankruptcies and defaults than there were in the 1960s and 1970s. The ability to analyze financial statements and make predictions regarding potential bankruptcies and defaults on bonds has always been important, but will increase in value in the future. To put it bluntly, the area of credit analysis will be a growth profession in the years ahead.

In this presentation I will review the studies that develop and test models to predict bankruptcies because these models can be useful to those who invest in the securities of distressed or bankrupt firms. I will begin with a review of the studies that used financial ratios to predict bankruptcy. The next section will discuss in some detail the Altman Z-score model because it is the most well-known financial ratio model and has stood the test of time. The third section deals with more recent studies that use cash flow variables to predict bankruptcy. Because most prior work used financial ratios, these recent studies have typically examined the impact of using cash flow variables in addition to financial ratios. I will conclude the presentation with a summary and conclusion regarding these results.

An Overview of the Research Methodology in Bankruptcy Studies

Anyone reviewing the research on this topic should recognize that bankruptcy prediction models are hindered by poor data. Typically, a fairly large sample of bankrupt companies is initially assembled, usually from 100 to 200 firms. There is invariably a problem obtaining enough data to perform the desired analysis. Generally, authors want to include data for five years prior to the bankruptcy to test how

early the failure can be predicted. The problem with requiring this much data is that either the data do not go back far enough or the company did not provide adequate financial statements for the final year before declaring bankruptcy. As an example, given an initial sample of 150 companies, the author may find only 30 companies with usable financial information. Hence, a sample of 40 or 50 companies is considered fairly large for a bankruptcy study, although it would be considered small for most other studies. The sample of bankrupt companies is matched with a comparable set of firms that did not go bankrupt, so that the researcher can test which financial ratios or cash flow variables will differentiate the firms that did not fail from the firms that did.

Financial Ratio Models

In the early studies, researchers developed bankruptcy prediction models that used financial ratios to discriminate between potential bankrupt and healthy firms. The **Appendix** contains a summary of the significant variables found in 14 studies that used financial ratios to predict failure and were published through the early 1980s. A summary of the ratios in these studies (**Table 1**) shows which ratios were the most significant in predicting failure.

The cash flow/total-debt ratio turns out to be a very good discriminator—even when a simplistic definition of cash flow is used. For example, in his 1966 study Beaver measured cash flow as simply net income plus depreciation and found it to be the best predictor of failure.

Table 1 also lists the general category for each of the most useful ratios which indicates what the ratio is attempting to measure, for example financial leverage or liquidity. As shown by this listing, which is based on the number of studies where ratios from alternative groups were significant, leverage and liquidity ratios tend to be the most useful for predicting failure, followed by several ratios that measure return on asset, cash position, and turnover. It is important to recognize that the significant ratios tend to vary between studies. In most cases, the researchers start with a fairly large number of ratios, and then winnow the list down to those that were statistically significant, as indicated by the statistical technique employed. Table 1 shows that a slightly different set of financial ratios was significant in each study, depending on the sample of firms or time period being examined.

Altman's Z-score Model

One of the best-known bankruptcy prediction models is Altman's Z-score model (Altman 1968). His model contains the following five variables: (1) a liquidity ratio, working capital as a percentage of total assets; (2) retained earnings divided by total assets, which may be interpreted as either an inverse leverage ratio of equity to total assets or a cumulative profitability ratio; (3) a profitability ratio, return on total assets; (4) a ratio of the market value of equity to the book value of debt, which is the inverse of the usual debt/equity leverage ratio; and (5) an efficiency ratio, sales divided by total assets.

The Z-score is computed using the coefficients obtained from a multiple discriminant analysis model.[1] The sum of the following computation is the Z-score:

Coefficient $\times$	Value of the Ratio
1.2 $\times$	(working capital/total assets)
+ 1.4 $\times$	(retained earnings/total assets)
+ 3.3 $\times$	(EBIT/total assets)
+ 0.6 $\times$	(market value of equity/book value of total liabilities)
+ 1.0 $\times$	(sales/total assets)

= Z-score

All the ratios are constructed so that a higher value for a specific ratio is better than a lower value. As an example, a higher proportion of working capital to total assets is a sign of greater liquidity. Therefore, the higher the value of the Z-score, the better off the company is and the lower the probability of bankruptcy.

The first step is to calculate Z-scores for a sample of firms that includes a set of firms that have declared bankruptcy and a matched set of similar firms that have not declared bankruptcy. The second step is to

[1]Discriminant analysis is a statistical technique that attempts to distinguish between groups on the basis of a set of characteristics (discriminating variables) on which the groups are hypothesized to differ.

determine the critical Z-score—that is, the Z-score that divides the sample into firms that are expected to go bankrupt and those that are not. This score is called the cutoff. In Altman's original sample, he found that none of the firms with Z-scores greater than 2.99 went bankrupt, but all those with Z-scores of less than 1.81 did. It was not possible to discriminate accurately for Z-scores between 1.81 and 2.99, but if a decision had to be made regarding a single cutoff value, the best critical value was specified to be 2.67.

Similar to other researchers, Altman was not able to obtain a large enough sample to withhold some of the failed companies to use in validating the model. Therefore, he classified firms in his original sample using the model developed from the same sample. Using the model one year before failure he was able to correctly predict bankruptcy in about 95 percent of the cases. The model was able to predict about 72 percent of failures two years prior to default. Those were considered fairly good results at the time.

It is important to recognize that the coefficients related to each of the ratio variables depend on the sample selected and on the time period. Specifically, a different set of firms at a different time will generate a different set of coefficients. Also, the Z-score cutoff value will change as the coefficients change.

Cash Flow Models

Much of the early work on predicting bankruptcy included only financial ratios. More recent studies have used cash flow values to predict bankruptcy. The most popular cash flow variable is cash flow from operations.

The following discussion considers several studies that have made significant contributions regarding the usefulness of cash flow. Because of the extensive work with financial ratios, most of the cash flow studies start with a financial ratio model, either Altman's or their own, and add one or several cash flow variables and attempt to measure the increase in predictability.[2]

Casey and Bartczak (1984, 1985) concluded that cash flow does not improve on the predictions of a financial ratio model. In one study (1984), the authors started with the best financial ratio model and added cash flow variables, mainly cash flow from operations. In a subsequent study (1985), they reached the same conclusion with a more extensive model.

Gentry, Newbold, and Whitford (1985a) tested a

[2]The sources of these studies are listed in the References, pp. 78-79.

Table 1. Summary of Most Useful Ratios for Predicting Failure by Factor Group

Factor Group/Ratio	Number of Studies in Which the Ratio Was Significant
Financial Leverage	
Cash Flow/Total Debt	7
Total Debt/Total Assets	6
Retained Earnings/Total Assets	5
Short-Term Liquidity	
Net Working Capital/Total Assets	6
Current Assets/Current Liabilities	6
Cash/Sales	2
Return on Investment	
Net Income/Total Assets	5
EBIT/Total Assets	4
Cash Position	
Cash/Current Liabilities	4
Receivables Turnover	
Quick Assets/Sales	2

Source: Gentry, Newbold, and Whitford (1984).

model with eight cash flow variables and found that the significant cash flow variable was dividends. This article confirmed the Casey and Bartczak assertion that cash flow does not add anything of significance because the addition of a cash flow variable (i.e., cash flow from operations) did not improve upon the best financial ratio model.

In a subsequent study (1985b), however, Gentry, Newbold, and Whitford extended their model from 8 to 12 variables by breaking up the working capital variable into its components so that it includes cash outflows to finance receivables and inventory. Their findings in this case were different from the results in the first study. Specifically, in this study there were three significant variables: cash outflows for dividends, investment, and receivables. A surprising result was that none of the cash inflow variables had a significant impact. Notably, cash flow from operations was not a significant variable. Because of this finding, cash outflow variables became very important to the bankruptcy analysis. Gentry, Newbold, and Whitford also found that a model that combined financial ratios and some cash flow variables was significantly better than either financial ratios or cash flows taken alone. When they started with the financial ratio model and added cash flow variables, the predictive ability increased significantly. The same was true when the financial ratios were added to a pure cash flow model. This approach was very different from the one-variable cash flow mod-

els that other studies had used.

Gombola, Haskins, Katz, and Williams (1987). Using multiple discriminant analysis and cash flow variables both before and after accruals, the authors found that the classification of cash flow variables changed over time. Specifically, when they used the model with data from the 1960s and early 1970s, they found that the cash flow variables tended to group with the income or investment variables instead of forming a separate class. More recently, the cash flow variables form a separate class. When the authors added the cash flow variable to the operating variables, they found that it did not significantly add to the ability to predict bankruptcy. This lack of significance is probably because they only used the "cash flow from operations" variable rather than the individual cash flow components.

Dambolena and Shulman (1988). In this study, the authors suggested that the net liquid balance variable is a significant addition to either a financial ratio model or a cash flow model. The net liquid balance variable equals the sum of cash and marketable securities minus short-term debt and current obligations on long-term debt. The authors used the Altman model as their financial ratio model and the Gentry, Newbold and Whitford model as the cash flow model. Adding the net liquid balance variable improved the performance of both models. With and without the net liquid balance variable, the Altman model gave better results than the Gentry-Newbold-Whitford model, although the latter showed more improvement with the addition of the net liquid balance variable. Both models were more accurate in classifying failed firms than they were in classifying firms that did not fail. This is an important and reassuring point for someone trying to predict bankruptcies among distressed firms. **Table 2** shows the results.

Aziz and Lawson (1989) tested many models, including the Altman Z-score model, the Altman zeta score model,[3] cash flow-based models like the Gentry-Newbold-Whitford model, and some models that were a mixture of the Z-score and cash flow models (referred to as mixed models). When Aziz and Lawson used the Z-score model, the coefficients and cutoffs were recomputed using updated data. They found that the cash flow and mixed models did not classify firms as failed or non-failed as successfully as the Z-score or zeta models did. On the other hand, the cash flow and mixed models did a better job of predicting failures. In other words, when attempting to predict bankruptcy one and two years before a failure, the authors experienced better re-

[3]See Altman, Haldeman, and Narayanan (1977).

Table 2. Classification Accuracy of Legal Bankruptcy Prediction Models

	Percentage of Firms Classified Correctly			
	Altman Model		*Gentry Model*	
	Without NLB	*With NLB*	*Without NLB*	*With NLB*
One Year Before Failure				
Failed Firms	98%	98%	86%	96%
Nonfailed Firms	72	86	62	82
Total	85	92	74	89
Two Years Before Failure				
Failed Firms	88%	88%	80%	84%
Nonfailed Firms	76	80	56	68
Total	82	84	68	76

NLB = Net liquid balance

Source: Dambolena and Shulman (1988).

sults with the cash flow-based and mixed models. The cash flow and mixed models tended to overpredict the number of failed firms. That is, when they erred, they erred on the conservative side, which is important to portfolio managers attempting to determine when to sell an issue.

Summary of Bankruptcy Prediction Studies

The studies in the 1970s and early 1980s relied heavily on the use of financial ratios to build predictive models. The ratio that provides the most consistent results is a very simplistic ratio of cash flow to total debt or cash flow to long-term debt. Altman's Z-score model has been the most consistent model over time. Although the coefficients and the cutoffs have changed depending on the sample and the time period, the original variables used in the Z-score model continue to be very useful.

Over the years, the trend has been toward the use of cash flow models, with a tendency to concentrate on the cash flow from operations variable. It appears that this concentration on one cash flow variable is a dangerous practice, because several studies have shown that adding only this cash flow variable to a financial ratio model does not produce much im-

provement. Put another way, studies have shown that the marginal contribution of the "cash flow from operations" variable to a financial ratio model is small.

The 12-variable cash flow model of Gentry, Newbold, and Whitford (1985b) has been shown to be significant and useful. A notable finding is that cash outflow variables were more significant in predicting bankruptcy than cash inflow variables. The usefulness of some of the cash flow variables will probably change when firms become involved in unusual transactions like the sale of assets or when a firm has accrued interest that is not paid.

An important characteristic of the Gentry-Newbold-Whitford cash flow model is that it is well specified and is based on standard accounting techniques. Because the variables are derived from the complete cash flow model, the 12 variables included in the model will not change. At the same time, the coefficients related to the individual cash flow variables and the cutoffs that signal problems will change. Different cash flow variables may be stressed at different times and under different circumstances, but the universe of cash flow variables will not change.

Conclusion

Cash flow and financial ratio models are very useful to investors interested in attempting to predict bankruptcy for a firm. The choice of a model depends on whether you prefer using financial ratios or cash flow variables. Remember, however, that the two sets of models are complementary, not competitive. In fact, most of the recent studies conclude that combining the models and using all the available information results in better predictions than relying solely on one model.

These models are also useful to investors in distressed-firm securities. The models can be used to predict recovery and track the firm's progress during the workout phase. By concentrating on the variables that showed significant deterioration prior to the bankruptcy, the investor or portfolio manager can see whether management is correcting the situation.

Appendix. Authors and Ratios for Fourteen Bankruptcy Studies*

Factor Group/ Ratios	Authors and Year of Study														Total
	Tarmari 1966	Beaver 1966	Altman 1968	Beaver 1968	Deakin 1972	Edmister 1972	Blum 1974	Elam 1975	Libby 1977	Altman 1977	Moyer 1977	Ohlson 1980	Taffler 1982	Menash 1983	
Receivables Turnover															
Size	X									X					2
S/Rec												X			1
QA/S					X		X								2
QA/INV							5								1
Inventory Turnover															
Prod/INV (1)	X														1
CGS/INV													X		1
NWC/S						4									1
S/WC	X														1
PROD/WC (1)						4									1
INV/S	X														1
CA/S					X				X						2
Cash Position															
C/S					X										1
C/TA					X										1
C/CL					X	4		X	X						4
No Cr. Int.				X											1
Quick Flow							6								1
Short-Term Liquidity															
QA/CL					X	4		X							3
CL/TA								X							1
C/TA									X						1
CA/CL	X			X	X			X	X	X		7			7
Financial Leverage															
BVEQ/TD							X								1
MVEQ/BVTD			X				X								2
CF/TD		X			X		X	X			X	5		X	7
CF/CL						4							X		2
WC/NW						4									1
CL/NW						4									1
TD/NW								X							1
MVCS/BVNW										X					1
TD/TA	2	X		X	X			X				X			6
RE/TA			X							X	X	X		X	5
INT/NI														X	1
EBIT/INT														X	1
Log EBIT/INT										X					1

Continued

27

Appendix. Authors and Ratios for Fourteen Bankruptcy Studies* (Continued)

Authors and Year of Study

Factor Group/ Ratios	Tarnari 1966	Beaver 1966	Altman 1968	Beaver 1968	Deakin 1972	Edmister 1972	Blum 1974	Elam 1975	Libby 1975	Altman 1977	Moyer 1977	Ohlson 1980	Taffler 1982	Menash 1983	Total
Capital Turnover															
S/FA														X	1
NW/S								X						X	2
CF/S				X				X							2
S/TA			X			X									2
NWC/TA		X	X	X	X						X	X			6
QA/TA					X						X				2
CA/TA									X				X		2
Return on Investments															
Tr. Breaks							X								1
Slope NI	3						X								2
EBIT/S								X							1
CF/NW								X						X	2
NI/NW							X	X							2
CF/TA				X											1
σ NI							X					X			2
σ EBIT/TA										X					1
NI/S								X							1
EBIT/TA			X					X		X	X				4
NI/TA		X			X				X			X	9		5

* A footnote number is sometimes substituted for an X.
1. Value of production = sales + finished goods + goods-in-process; ratio not included in Chen and Shimerda (18).
2. Used TL in denominator.
3. Trend of net income, combined with NI/TA for one category of index to risk.
4. Company ratio/industry ratio.
5. Standard deviation, trend breaks and slope of the QA/S ratio.
6. Quick flow = C + N.Rec. + ms + (S/12) CGS − Deprec. + S&Admin Expense + Interest. A trend break occurs when the performance of a variable declines between year t and t+1.
7. Inverse, i.e., CL/CA.
8. CF = funds provided by operations.
9. TA_{t-1}

CA	Current assets	QA	Quick assets
TA	Total assets	NI	Net income
NWC	Net working capital	S	Sales
Rec	Receivables	PROD	Cost of production
TL	Total loss	MVEQ	Market value of equity
BVTD	Book value total debt	MVCS	Market value common stock
BVNW	Book value of net worth	EBIT	Earnings before interest and taxes
No. Cr. Int.	Number of credit intervals		
FA	Fixed assets		
CL	Current liabilities		
C	Cash		
INV	Inventory		
BVEQ	Book value of equity		
NW	Net worth		
RE	Retained earnings		
Tr. Breaks	Breaks in trend		

Source: Gentry, Newbold, and Whitford (1984).

Question and Answer Session

Question: Did the researchers include retiree medical obligations and pension deficiencies in their ratios?

Reilly: If the sample firm had to make specific payments for retiree medical obligations and pension deficiencies, these would be picked up in the cash flows. If, however, these costs were being accrued, they would not show up in the cash flows. It is a question of whether the obligations are being paid or simply accrued. Clearly, if there is an obligation it should be included.

Question: Can the Z-score be used in the case of a highly leveraged LBO in which there are no retained earnings, and thus no real equity, after the balance sheet has been adjusted?

Reilly: Yes. Note that in the original model, there is a variable for market value of equity over the book value of debt. So, if the company is public, even though the balance sheet shows negative equity there will still be a market value. Kroger is one example of this situation. Altman also tested the model using book value with private firms (Altman 1983). In this case, the ratio values would be negative. Nevertheless, if the sample is defined correctly—that is, all private firms—the model should still differentiate between the failed and non-failed firms. Of course, the coefficients and cutoffs would be different.

Question: Why bother with any of these models?

Why not do a five-year projection of the company's financial needs and then assess its ability to tap the capital markets?

Reilly: That is a wonderful idea if you are in a position to make such a projection. The point is that most analysts or portfolio managers are not able to do this, so they must rely on historical data to help in this projection. Another use of these models is to pinpoint those companies that probably will have trouble and then concentrate on attempting your five-year projection for that smaller set of firms rather than trying to do it for every firm.

Question: Does the Z-score model work equally well for all industries? For example, is the model appropriate for financial institutions?

Reilly: The concept is relevant for all industrial firms, but it may not be practical to compare firms across all industries using one set of variables and coefficients. Certainly the coefficients for the variable will vary by specific industries or industry groups, such as heavy industrial companies versus retail firms versus service firms (this is especially true for the asset turnover ratio, which varies widely for different industry groups). In some cases, the variables (i.e., the specific ratios) may also differ. Financial institutions and utilities are examples of industries where even the variables (the ratios included in the model) might change because of significant differences in their balance sheets and income statements relative to other industries.

Covenants: What Kind of Protection Do They Offer?

Richard S. Wilson
Managing Director, Research Products and Services
Fitch Investors Service, Inc.

Bond covenants and the bondholder/stockholder, creditor/debtor conflict have increasingly captured the attention of bond market participants in the past several years. Despite the rising interest, covenant protection for bondholders has deteriorated over the past decade. Recently, however, covenants have been receiving increased attention by participants in both the high-grade and junk bond market.

Not everyone believes that covenants are of concern to investors. For example, Graham and Dodd state that "the primary aim of the bond investor must be to avoid trouble rather than to seek protection in the event of trouble."[1] One easy way to avoid trouble is to take Polonius's advice: "Neither a borrower, nor a lender be." In other words, refrain from investing in corporate bonds. Of course, this is not a realistic option for most investment professionals.

For those of us who cannot refrain from investing in corporate bonds, it is important to understand the role of covenants. We are dealing with living entities affected by all types of events, some of which may not be of their own choosing. Knowledge is power, and the informed bond investor has a better chance of avoiding costly mistakes.

In this presentation I will discuss covenants and address several questions that investors have been asking. Do investors really care about the terms of the bond contract other than the yield? Are covenants necessary and useful? Are bondholders getting what they pay for in bond contracts?

Indenture Provisions and Covenants

An indenture is a legal document connected with a debt issue that details the rights and obligations of the lender and borrower. Some indentures are relatively simple; others can be quite complex, running into hundreds of pages. Billions of dollars of public corporate bonds change hands every day, but many of the participants are unaware of the terms of the bond contracts they trade. Although more market participants are familiar with issue terms than was the case 10 years ago, others are still ignorant, knowing not much more than the coupon, the maturity, and possibly some of the redemption terms. Maybe that is all one needs to know as long as the company stays out of trouble.

Indentures contain both affirmative covenants and negative or restrictive covenants. Affirmative covenants call for the debtor to take certain actions: to pay interest, principal, and premium, if any, on a timely basis, and pay all taxes and other claims when due unless contested in good faith. The debtor must maintain all properties used and useful in its business in good condition and working order, and maintain its corporate existence, among other obligations.

Negative covenants prohibit the borrower from taking certain actions. They include limitations on the issuance of additional debt, because unrestricted borrowing can lead a company and its debtholders to ruination. Interest-coverage tests, dividend restrictions, and prohibitions on the use of proceeds from asset sales are other negative covenants. These protect investors from management dissipating a company's assets at the expense of bondholders.

The Decline in Covenant Protection

Over the past couple of decades, American bondholders have acquiesced to declining covenant protection. This is illustrated by the last three issues of KN Energy, Inc. (formerly Kansas-Nebraska Natural Gas Company, Inc.). KN Energy publicly offered debentures in 1976, 1982, and 1988, under three separate (and progressively weaker) indentures. The 1976 and 1982 issues had dividend-payment and share-repurchase limitations; the 1988 issue did not. The debt-issuance capitalization test under the 1976 and 1982 indentures limited debt to

---

[1]Cottle, Sidney, Roger F. Murray, and Frank E. Block. 1988. *Graham and Dodd's Security Analysis*, Fifth Edition (p. 447). New York: McGraw-Hill Book Company.

no more than 60 percent of pro forma capitalization; there was no limiting provision in the 1988 indenture. The 1976 issue provided for an interest-coverage test for debt issuance that was not in the 1982 and 1988 indentures.

In some cases there may even be an absence of restrictive covenants. It is as though companies are saying, "Give me your money and I will do as I please with it. You'd better hope that I use it profitably because if I don't, I may come back and offer you 40 or 50 cents (or less) on the dollar so I can continue in this charade." The alternative could be a time-consuming bankruptcy that may get you less than an out-of-court restructuring.

The current sentiment is illustrated in the Transamerica Finance Group, Inc. prospectus, dated October 4, 1989, which states:

> The Indentures do not contain any provision which will restrict the Company in any way from paying dividends or making other distribution on its capital stock or purchasing or redeeming any of its capital stock, or from incurring, assuming, or becoming liable upon Senior Indebtedness, Subordinated Indebtedness or Junior Subordinated Indebtedness or any other type of debt or other obligations. The Indentures do not contain any financial ratios or specified levels of net worth or liquidity to which the company must adhere. In addition, the Subordinated and Junior Subordinated Indentures do not restrict the Company from creating liens on its property for any purpose.[2]

Negative pledge clauses have long provided protection for senior unsecured debt by limiting a company's ability to create or assume a lien (subject to certain exceptions) without equally securing the unsecured debt. The amount of mortgage or secured debt, usually limited to 5 percent of consolidated net worth, has in recent years been raised in a number of cases to 10 percent, and even as much as 15 percent. Will the blue sky be the next limit?

There are a number of reasons why issuers ask for indenture changes or amendments, including making the indenture conform with changing corporate law and practices. An issuer may be close to covenant violations and need bondholders' waivers. Changes may grant management more leeway and financial flexibility, allowing them to do things that they had not been able to do before. They may even grant management too much flexibility.

Less restraint on corporate managements might mean more problems for debtholders in the future.

At a recent bondholder rights meeting in New York it was noted, however, that there has been improvement in covenants of some speculative-grade debt issues. The test lies ahead as more debtors who sold bonds in the past 10 years meet with financial difficulty. They may have to restructure or die!

Are Covenants Useful?

Despite considerable criticism to the contrary, covenants *do* work. This is demonstrated by the number of issues that have been redeemed or defeased prior to management taking steps that would weaken the debt if it were to remain outstanding. For example, XTRA Inc. recently redeemed its Series A medium-term notes under the event-risk covenant because of a change in control and a downgrading to below investment grade.

In addition, covenants have value. In fact, some issuers have paid bondholders to change covenant provisions, as the recent Armco Inc. solicitation demonstrates. Armco offered $10 per note for holders to consent to an amendment to the indenture, which would allow it to continue to pay common stock dividends.

It should be noted that covenants do not always work. They do not work when they are loosely written, such as some of the early poison puts, because management will take advantage of every loophole in the contract if it is to the issuer's benefit. Covenants do not work when pusillanimous investors sit back and allow managements to ride all over them. For this reason, it is important for investors to understand covenants.

Areas for Improvement in Covenants

An important area of bondholder concern is adequate disclosure and the flow of information. There has been some improvement in recent years, but much still needs to be done. Several areas of improvement in covenants are outlined below.

It is essential in publicly issued bond indentures that proper covenant language ensures the flow of information to the market. A 1975 *New York Times* article stated that bondholders, treated as second-class citizens, are entitled to the same flow of information that is provided to stockholders.[3] Many issuers do not do this. This is especially so in cases of privately owned companies issuing public debt.

---

[2]Prospectus for $100,000,000 Transamerica Finance Group, Inc. 8-3/4% Notes Due 1999. (October 4, 1989)

[3]"Tell It to the Bondholder, Too," *New York Times*, May 18, 1975. See also "When Companies Conceal the Facts," *New York Times*, September 14, 1990.

They only have to make financial filings with the Securities and Exchange Commission (SEC) for the first year. After that, if there are fewer than 300 security holders of record, they may choose not to file. This is a real problem because many bond issues are held by fewer than 300 holders. Although institutions have many beneficial owners of a particular issue, the bonds are registered in one nominee name.

The covenants should require that issuers of publicly offered bonds provide timely quarterly and annual reports to bondholders, potential bondholders, their authorized agents, and nationally recognized statistical rating organizations. These reports should be the type companies would have to file with the SEC if they were subject to the reporting requirements, as long as the bonds are outstanding. Also, the reports should have a special covenant section outlining the company's compliance with any special ratios and financial provisions, and calculating the ratios and statistics according to the language of the particular covenants.

A number of people have proposed guidelines for covenants. For example, Richard Weinberg of Reliance Group Holdings prepared a list of covenant proposals that investors should strive for.[4] These include:

- stronger debt-incurrence tests with fewer exceptions;
- limits on the issuance of senior debt with restrictions reaching down to subsidiary preferred, which would be structurally senior to the debt of their parent;
- tighter covenants concerning restricted payments, including limits on loans, advances, and investments in affiliates;
- maintenance of net worth clause in all future debt issues;
- restrictions on the ability of an issuer to sell assets;
- restrictions on how the proceeds of asset sales are used;
- stronger merger covenants and tests; for example, the test should require consolidated fixed-charge coverage and tangible net worth after the merger to be not less than it was prior to the merger; and
- covenants that cover affiliated party transactions, trustees, and tax sharing.

This is just a starting point. You will be hearing more about these and other proposals in the years ahead. Pay attention, and let managements know your views. Get them to improve their bondholder communications. After all, bondholders provide a large amount of capital to these people and deserve a fair shake.

The Three C's of Credit

Investors should remember the three C's of credit before buying a bond issue, not afterward. They are:

1. *Character* of the issuer and its people. "A man's word is his bond" is no longer applicable in this modern world (if indeed it ever was). If investors lend money to companies with unsavory management, they probably deserve to get burned.
2. *Capacity* of the issuer to repay its debts. Certainly, very highly leveraged companies may have more difficulty meeting their obligations than those with less debt, especially under difficult economic conditions.
3. *Collateral*—the lender's relative position to the collateral, from fully secured to junior debt positions.

Covenants can affect the C's. Graham and Dodd said, "safety is measured by the issuer's ability to meet *all* its obligations under adverse economic and financial conditions, not by the contractual terms of the specific issue."[5] This is so because when a business fails, there is shrinkage of asset values. Further, there may be difficulty in asserting the bondholders' supposed legal rights. Finally, there are delays, costs, and other disadvantages of a receivership or bankruptcy. LTV went into Chapter 11 more than four years ago and management still has not even filed a proposed reorganization statement. Legal conflict over the pension fund is a big contributor to this delay.

Certainly, covenants cannot make a good credit out of a bad one. There are no alchemists that can turn a sow's ear into a silk purse. Analysts and portfolio managers must perform proper indenture and credit analysis, and due diligence. It takes time, but bond analysis is a negative art. Good art, like good wine, does not occur overnight. Lack of proper covenants, however, can change good credits into LDCs (less desirable credits). We have seen much of that in the 1980s; let's hope that in the 1990s investors will fare better.

To aid investors, rating agencies and others provide services covering indenture analysis. For example, Standard & Poor's Corporation has an event-

---

[4] From a presentation to the Bondholder Rights Committee, Association for Investment Management and Research, July 19, 1990.

[5] *Graham and Dodd's Security Analysis, op. cit.,* p. 442.

risk rating. It has also developed a covenant ranking for Rule 144a private placements. Fitch Investors Service has a covenant analysis service for publicly issued high-yield bonds. The reports summarize the major covenants of an issue, and give a covenant ranking and opinion. The indenture opinion assesses the degree of covenant protection provided. The opinion evaluates the vulnerability of creditworthiness resulting from events such as recapitalizations, mergers, takeovers, and changes in a company's financial strategy involving asset sales, dividend payments, and debt issuance.

Conclusion

To paraphrase William Henry Vanderbilt, "The bondholder be damned; I am working for my stockholders." Bond investors must be wary. The relationship between a creditor and a debtor is contractual. Corporate managements and boards of directors are not fiduciaries for all investors in the enterprise; if they were, many restrictive covenants would be unnecessary. Management's primary responsibility is to increase shareholder wealth (or their own), not the wealth of the total firm. This can be done at bondholders' expense. Until the courts and state legislatures act to protect bondholders, consideration must be given to the resurrection of good, old-fashioned, well-written, and thorough restrictive provisions.

You get what you pay for. If investors want better covenant protection, they must pay for it. Why should management grant bondholders more than they have to without adequate consideration in return? Investment bankers do not act as moral trustees for public bondholders in the shaping of covenants, as some may have done in a bygone age. Bankers get paid by the issuers, so make them earn their pay. Point out to the issuers through their bankers that you want certain types of covenants and are willing to reduce the coupon by 25 or 50 basis points or so. Be willing to negotiate. You may not get all that you want, but if you do not ask, you may never receive.

A cry heard several years ago was, "Bondholders of the world, unite!" After years of declining interest in covenants, bondholders, tired of having sand kicked in their faces, have awakened and are taking steps to redress their grievances. In 1987 the Institutional Bondholders Rights Association was formed to review the needs of bond investors in the covenant field and to discuss the findings with other investors, investment bankers, and issuers. Earlier in 1977 another group, the Fixed Income Analysts Society, Inc. in New York, presented testimony to the SEC concerning covenant-related matters. The membership later approved two resolutions on fiduciary duties to bondholders and adequate financial disclosure. Last, but not least, the Association for Investment Management and Research formed the Bondholder Rights Committee in New York. This group has held several meetings and is setting up focus groups to study and report on disclosure, exchange offers and restructuring, covenants, bondholder proxies, and trustee responsibilities, among other topics.

Finally, remember TNSTAAFL: There's no such thing as a free lunch!

Question and Answer Session

Question: Do you expect private-placement covenants to weaken with the advent of Rule 144?

Wilson: I don't think covenants will weaken with the advent of Rule 144 because I think investors have learned a few lessons about covenant protection—or lack of protection. Certainly Metropolitan Life will be demanding better covenants. Unfortunately, as long as there is more demand for a particular issue than the number of bonds out there, the issuer can get away with weak covenants. There will still be deals sold without what you consider to be adequate covenants, but you don't have to buy them. I think investors will demand more from issuers in the covenants.

Question: To what extent should bondholders be compensated for granting waivers or changes in covenants?

Wilson: Currently, there are no set guidelines for how much to pay for granting waivers or changes in covenants. Large investors have an advantage because they can use their market power to negotiate compensation. With time, experience will provide an indication of what they are worth. Standard & Poor's started reviewing how many basis points event risk or poison puts saved the company. In the beginning these covenants were worth about 25 or 35 basis points. Recently investors are not caring very much about poison puts, so they are not valuing

them at all. It depends on the interest in the market, and the amount of takeovers in the merger activity in that particular case. Academics should start working on this problem.

Question: Do covenants help a junior subordinated bondholder?

Wilson: A junior subordinated bondholder's protection is typically pretty weak because he is so low in seniority, although the actual experience depends on the circumstances of the company. If they are covered by covenants and as long as the company has not gone belly-up, the issuer has to pay some attention to the subordinated bondholders. The junk market today is basically a market of subordinated issues with a lot less protection for the bondholder.

Question: With the tremendous size of the junk bond market, and this great deficiency in quality of information communicated to the investor, how can we collectively get a better deal in terms of timeliness and completeness of information?

Wilson: Start by communicating with your investment bankers, the bond issuers, and the SEC. Second, join bondholder rights groups. Join the AIMR group if you are in New York, or the Association of Institutional Bondholders. This is an equity-oriented world. Bondholders must unite, otherwise we are going to all hang separately.

The Market for Distressed and Defaulted Securities

Edward I. Altman
Max L. Heine Professor of Finance
New York University

The substantial increase in the supply and diversity of bankrupt and near-bankrupt companies, and the perceived sizeable upside potential of securities selling at deeply discounted prices, is attracting investors to this area. When I began studying distressed companies 25 years ago, very few people analyzing corporate activity would even look at troubled companies. Only a few specialists, such as bankruptcy lawyers and bank workout analysts, were interested. The distressed-firm area was not very important to organizations in the 1960s, '70s, and early '80s. In fact, if you worked in a bank and were placed in the workout department or given the job of following distressed loans, it was an indication that your banking career was finished.

Dramatic changes have occurred. Now, good analysts of distressed companies are considered to be very valuable employees. Although many areas of the investment industry are not doing very well, the demand for the services of lawyers and analysts in the bankruptcy field is booming. It may seem perverse to be enthusiastic about failures, but for those in the business, times are good.

In this presentation, I will review the findings of my study of the market for distressed securities (see Altman 1990). The purpose of the study is to document and analyze this unique asset class, both in terms of a descriptive anatomy of the market's major characteristics and participants and an analytical treatment of its pricing dynamics and performance attributes.

The Size of the Distressed Securities Market

The study begins with a summary of the distressed securities debt market. The size of this market depends on its definition. Distressed securities may be narrowly defined as only those publicly held debt and equity securities of firms that have defaulted on their debt obligations and/or have filed for protection under Chapter 11 of the Bankruptcy Code. A more comprehensive definition would encompass those publicly held debt securities selling at prices that are discounted enough that the securities yield a significant premium over U.S. Treasury bonds and private bank and trade debt of those same companies.

If the comprehensive definition is used, the size of the market is estimated to have a book value of $301 billion and a market value of $202 billion. **Table 1** presents the estimated public and private debt outstanding of defaulted and distressed firms as of January 31, 1990.

Defaulted securities are defined as the defaulted debt and equity securities of publicly traded corporations as well as defaulted privately traded securities. The private debt market is an increasingly important part of the distressed securities market. In addition, it has a fair amount of inefficiency, so there are opportunities for extraordinary returns. The private debt market includes bank debt, trade claims, and other notes and paper.

The size of the publicly traded defaulted debt market in January 1990 was estimated to be $11.5 billion (market value) and $26 billion (par value). The ratio of market value to book value was about 44 percent. The defaulted debt market in December 1990 was probably close to $16 billion. In January 1990, the book value of distressed, but not defaulted, debt was estimated to be $50 billion, with a market value of $33 billion. This gives a market-to-book-value ratio of 66 percent. So the totals for publicly traded securities are $76 billion of book value and $45 billion of market value.

Distressed debt is defined as any bond selling for a current yield at least 10 percentage points greater than the risk-free rate on a security of comparable maturity. For example, with the long-term government bond rate approaching 9 percent and the 10-year Treasury rate around 8.8 percent, a distressed security would be defined as one that has a current yield of 19 percent or more. This is obviously an

Table 1. Estimated Public and Private Debt Outstanding of Defaulted and Distressed Firms as of January 31, 1990

	Book Value ($ billions)	Market Value ($ billions)	Market/Book Ratio
Publicly Traded			
Defaulted Debt	$26.0	$11.5	0.44
Distressed Debt	50.0	33.0	0.66
	$76.0	$44.5	
Privately Placed			
Defaulted Debt	$ 75.0	$ 45.0	0.60
Distressed Debt	150.0	112.5	0.75
	$225.0	$157.5	
Total Public & Private	$301.0	$202.0	0.67

Source: Altman (1990).

arbitrary definition. Some people define a distressed security as one that sells for 60 or 70 cents on the dollar, but this is not an acceptable definition because there are many original-issue discount bonds that normally sell at these levels. Also, a definition framed in this way would require much more research into security prices.

The private debt market includes private debt with public registration rights, private bank debt, and trade claims of defaulted and distressed companies. This market is considerably larger than the public market, but its size cannot be as reliably estimated as the public market because data are not readily available and maintained

One approach to estimating the size of the private market is to use the relation between private debt and public debt of distressed and defaulted companies. To estimate the ratio of private to public debt, we examined the capital structures of 103 bankrupt firms. The ratio was 3.8:1. Of these 103 firms, 68 companies had public debt in addition to private debt. The ratio for these firms was 3.1:1. The distribution of the ratio of private to public debt of 68 large bankrupt companies with both private and public debt is shown in **Table 2**.

Another way of looking at the problem is to examine the capital structures of leveraged buyouts financed by junk bonds. **Figure 1** shows that during 1987 and 1988, around 60 percent of financing came from bank debt and other senior debt. Another 20 percent was raised with subordinated coupon debt, and 7 percent with deferred interest bonds, payment-in-kind bonds, and similar instruments. So, assuming that most of the senior debt was private, the ratio obtained from looking at the capital structure is a little less than 3:1. Therefore, it seems fairly safe to use a ratio of 3:1 as an estimate of private

to public debt for distressed companies. In other words, for every $1 in book value of publicly traded debt, there are $3 in book value of privately placed debt.

Estimates of the total size of the market are obtained by tripling the size of the public debt. Thus, the defaulted private debt market was estimated to be $75 billion, and the distressed private debt market $150 billion. This results in estimate of $300 billion for total public and private debt. The market value of this debt is approximately $200 billion, so the market-to-book ratio is 67 percent on average.

Although these total figures do not mean very much unless the components are examined individually, it is clear that the market is very large and growing. By December 1990, the market had probably grown to $350 billion or more.

Trend in Recovery Rates

An investor interested in buying the securities of companies that default would probably want to know the trend in recovery value (price after default) for those distressed securities. Over the past 50 to 60 years, bonds consistently sold for about 40 percent of par value just after default. **Table 3** shows recovery rates on defaulted debt by seniority from 1985 to 1989. For the five years from 1985 to 1989, secured senior debt tended to sell for 66 percent of par, senior debt for 55 percent of par, senior subordinated debt for 31.6 percent of par, and subordinated debt for 32.1 percent of par.

It may seem an anomaly that the subordinated debt sold at higher prices than the senior subordinated debt. This can be explained by noting that in some cases there may have been no senior subordinated debt, so this debt would have the lowest

Table 2. Distribution of the Ratio of Private to Public Debt of Large Bankrupt Companies

Ratio	Number of Companies	Percent of Total
0 – 1.9	14	21%
2.0 – 3.9	16	24
4.0 – 5.9	9	13
6.0 – 7.9	10	15
8.0 – 9.9	5	7
10.0 –11.9	4	6
12.0 –13.9	2	3
14.0 –15.9	2	3
16.0 –17.9	1	1
18.0 –19.9	0	0
>= 20.0	5	7
	68	100%

Source: Compilation by E. Altman.

Figure 1. Capital Structures of LBOs Financed by Junk Bonds

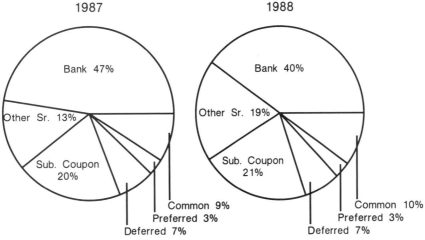

priority. Also, the samples used in the calculations are different. In finding the average for the senior subordinated debt, 53 issues were used, whereas 100 were used in calculating the subordinated debt average.

It is interesting to note that the 1989 recovery rate is less than 25 percent for the senior subordinated and subordinated debt. An investor who bought those bonds at par and sold them just after default would have received less than 25 cents for each dollar invested. Although the sample size is small, it seems that there is a deterioration in recovery values, particularly for lower seniorities.

The attractiveness of an investment is influenced by the probability of bankruptcy. **Figure 2** shows the proportion of the S&P industrials with Z-scores below 1.81. A Z-score less than 1.81 has been found to correspond to a significantly high probability of bankruptcy. As shown, the low point was reached

at the end of 1979 when 3 percent of the S&P industrials had Z-scores below the critical value. In the latest calculation in 1989, 10 percent had scores below 1.81, which is disturbing. However, 9 percent of companies were below 1.81 in the recession of 1974, so figures this high are not unprecedented. Nevertheless, this is one indication that the distress is not yet over, and that defaults will continue at a high level for several more years.

Distressed Security Investor Profile

The study also includes a survey of investors in distressed securities. The firms included in the survey were those that decided to invest a high proportion of their funds in distressed or defaulted securities; they were not junk bond funds that are compelled to invest in that area. Of the 85 questionnaires

Table 3. Recovery Rates* on Defaulted Debt by Seniority (1985-89)

Year	Secured		Senior		Senior Subordinated		Subordinated	
1989	$82.69	(9)	$53.70	(16)	$21.53	(18)	$24.56	(29)
1988	67.96	(13)	41.59	(20)	29.23	(11)	36.42	(18)
1987	12.00	(1)	70.52**	(29)	51.22	(9)	40.54	(7)
1986	48.32	(7)	40.84	(7)	31.53	(8)	30.95	(33)
1985	74.25	(2)	34.81	(2)	36.18	(7)	41.45	(13)
Arith. Avg.	$66.451	(32)	$55.292**	(74)	$31.614	(53)	$32.118	(100)

(Number of issues)
* Price per $100 par value at end of default month.
** Without Texaco, 1987 Recovery = $29.77
Arithmetic Average Senior Recovery = $43.11

Source: Compilation by E. Altman and D. Chin, New York University

Figure 2. Chance of Bankruptcy within S&P Industrials**

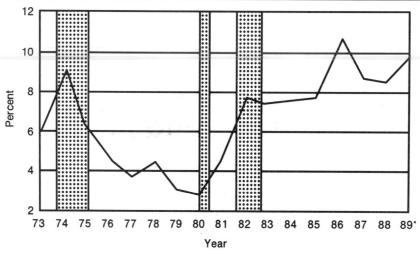

Shaded Areas are NBER Recession Periods. (*) 1989 Data are Latest 4 Qtrs.
** Percent of S&P Industrials with Z-scores <=1.81.

Source: Bernstein, Richard. "Quantitative Viewpoint." Merrill Lynch & Co. Global Securities Research & Economics Group. (December 1990.)

sent out, there were 56 responses.

The survey results indicate that there is at least $5 billion under active management by investment firms dedicated to the distressed securities field. The amount of money under management in distressed securities in the sample ranges from less than $20 million to more than $300 million. **Table 4** presents the distribution of invested dollars among distressed investor institutions. Of the responding companies that indicated their dollar commitment to distressed securities investing, only two firms had $300 million or more under management, 11 firms had between $100 and $300 million under management, and 24 firms had less than $50 million under management. At least two additional investment vehicles have been recently formed with available funds greater than $200 million.

Many of the firms are relatively new to the field, as **Table 5** shows. Eighteen of the firms have been in

business for less than two years. This does not necessarily mean that they are inexperienced; it is probably the result of money managers from other companies or workout people from banks deciding to start their own firms. Seven firms have been in the industry, which is actually a niche within money management, for 20 years or more. These people have generally done very well, but, as a result, they now have much more competition.

Table 5. Distribution of Years in Business of Distressed Investors as of December 1989

Years in Business	Number of Investors	Percent of Investors
<1	8	15%
1 – 2	10	18
3	7	13
4	2	4
5	6	11
6 – 10	6	11
11 – 15	9	16
16 – 20	0	0
>20	7	12
Total	55	100%

Source: Compilation by E. Altman. See Altman (1991).

The risky nature of the business, the relatively poor liquidity of the issues, and the costly skills required to analyze investments in this area lead investors to require a high minimum rate of return. To determine how high the minimum is, the survey queried respondents about target and minimum annual rates of return to investors. **Table 6** presents the

Table 4. Distribution of Invested Dollars among Distressed Investor Institutions

Amount under Management in Distressed Securities (in $ millions)	Number of Firms	Percent of Firms
$ 0 – 20	11	22%
21 – 50	13	26
51 – 100	13	26
101 – 300	11	22
301 – 500	2	4
Total	50	100%

Source: Compilation by E. Altman. See Altman (1991).

results. Of the 49 respondents, 27 had target rates of return of 25 or 30 percent. A few had less, and 18 had target rates of 35 percent or more. Many of the firms are private partnerships that raise money, with fixed time periods and very high target rates of return. The majority of minimum rates of return were in the range of 20 to 30 percent. Because investors in distressed securities are similar to equity funds with high average portfolio betas, very few have target rates of less than 20 percent. They cannot attract very many investors who are happy with 15 percent returns.

There have been several other studies on the returns to investing in defaulted and distressed securities. Hradsky and Long (1989) published a study on the cumulative excess returns on defaulted debt securities (see **Figure 3**). Returns were examined for the period two years before and two years after a bankruptcy or default. The cumulative excess return was then calculated by taking the total return on the defaulted security and subtracting the amount that could have been earned on a junk bond portfolio over a comparable period. The Blume-Keim high yield debt index was used as a proxy for the junk bond portfolio. Hradsky and Long found that the excess, or residual, return on distressed securities is close to zero until about 10 months prior to the default. Then, if an investor holds onto the bonds as default approaches, the cumulative excess return drops to –40 percent. This means that an investor would have lost about 40 percent of his money over the 10-month period before bankruptcy or default.

These results have implications for when investors should buy distressed securities. Some investors are interested in the period before default because they see the possibility of a great buying opportunity. This may not be a good strategy, because on average the negative excess returns have historically continued right to the default date. The more interesting result, however, is the continued decline in the excess return after the bankruptcy date. For the first six months after default, investors continue to get hurt.

Excess returns drop another 7 to 8 percent, with a bottom finally reached 6 months after the default occurred. This probably happens because it takes time for people to get a feel for the financing and the particulars of a bankrupt firm's situation.

Storage Technology is a good example of a company that provided easily obtained excess returns. Their bonds were selling at 45 cents on the dollar just after default, but the firm had very good assets. Some investors saw that the liabilities would be worth 70 to 80 percent of par at a minimum, and all that they needed to do was hold the bonds long enough. In fact, the bonds went to 135 percent of par within two to three years. Unfortunately, there are not many cases that are this easy. Nevertheless, it is important for the potential investor to have analyzed the securities and assets before the opportunity arises. After the bottom at six months after default, the excess returns rise, then drop again.

Remember that these are excess or residual returns, not total returns. Total returns may not have been negative; only the premium over the high-yield index became negative. It is an interesting finding that, during the reorganization, investors start making money relative to their opportunity cost from the sixth month to the tenth month, but then start to lose again between the tenth and sixteenth months after default.

Investment Strategies

Several studies on bankrupt equity securities have shown that returns from firms achieving a successful reorganization were exceptionally high, but that for the entire sample the overall return was about equal to relevant equity opportunity costs.

In the Altman/Foothill report (1990), I concentrated on the returns to distressed rather than defaulted securities, whereby a distressed security was defined as one with a current yield at least 10 percentage points over the comparable Treasury-

Figure 3. Cumulative Excess Returns on Defaults Only (1977-88)

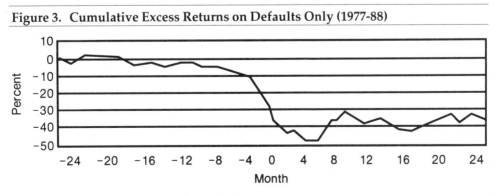

Source: Hradsky and Long (1989).

Table 6. Target and Minimum Rates of Return on Distressed Securities Investing

Target Rate of Return	Respondents Number	Respondents Percent	Minimum Rate of Return	Respondents Number	Respondents Percent
<20%	0	0%	<20%	2	4%
20	4	8	20	15	31
25	11	23	25	16	33
30	16	33	30	10	20
35	5	10	35	4	8
40	9	18	40	2	4
>40	4	8	>40	0	0
Total	49	100%		47	100%

Source: Compilation by E. Altman. See Altman (1991).

bond rate. My Zeta model—the second generation Z-score model—was used to categorize companies based on their creditworthiness. The Zeta model has seven variables, five of which are similar to the Z-score model; it also includes a variable on stability of earnings and a variable on the size of the company. The securities were then tracked for 36 months after first being defined as distressed. The sample includes 310 observations over the period 1978 to 1989. **Table 7** presents the results.

As Panel A shows, a strategy of investing in all high-yield-spread issues would have earned an average gross return of 35.2 percent over three-year periods. Compared to a comparable junk bond portfolio, this portfolio would have lost 18 percent,

so blindly investing in every distressed security was not a good strategy. If an investor had been able to avoid all defaults (Panel B), he could have earned exceptionally high returns (29.7 percent, 67.6 percent, and 90.3 percent for one- two-, and three-year periods, respectively), with a positive residual around 27 percent for the three-year period.

It is obviously close to impossible to avoid all the bonds that will go into default, but it may be possible to avoid a fair number of them and obtain very good returns. When the investor chose only those companies with positive Zeta values, the return increased to 79.1 percent over three-year periods. There were only 10 observations, however, which is a fairly small number. This model is probably not

Table 7. Performance Results for Various Strategies of Investing in Distressed Debt Securities (1978-89)

	Gross Return (%) Months After Distress						Residual Return (%) Months After Distress					
	6	12	19	24	30	36	6	12	18	24	30	36
A. Invest in All High-Yield-Spread Issues												
Return	(7.2)	2.0	9.2	22.7	29.6	35.2	(14.1)	(15.2)	(16.4)	(9.7)	(12.5)	(18.1)
No. of Issues	310	251	199	160	114	83	310	251	199	160	114	83
Significant	(.05)*						Yes	Yes	Yes	No	Yes	Yes
B. Invest in All Nondefaulting High-Yield-Spread Issues												
Return	7.1	29.7	45.4	67.6	80.2	90.3	0.4	10.5	14.8	30.1	28.6	26.8
No. of Issues	132	93	76	67	49	39	132	93	76	67	49	39
Significant	(.05)*						No	Yes	Yes	Yes	Yes	Yes
C. Invest in Positive Zeta Distressed High-Yield Issues												
Return	15.4	23.6	45.7	43.2	68.1	79.1	3.1	1.1	15.1	8.1	22.1	22.7
No. of Issues	10	9	9	9	8	8	10	9	9	9	8	8
Significant	(.05)*						No	No	No	No	No	No
D. Invest in Zeta –1 Distressed High-Yield Issues												
Return	17.6	24.2	37.3	44.9	68.4	72.9	5.4	1.0	7.9	9.8	20.7	23.8
No. of Issues	31	29	26	24	17	16	31	29	26	24	17	16
Significant	(.05)*						No	No	No	No	Yes	No

* $t = \dfrac{\bar{x}}{6/\sqrt{N}}$, at .05 level, approximately 2.

Source: Compilation by E. Altman and T. Ng, New York University

very much help to large money managers with hundreds of millions of dollars to invest, because it presents too few investment opportunities. So, the cutoff was relaxed to –1, which enabled us to include slightly distressed companies. Although the sample was still fairly small, it increased to 31 securities. The average B-rated company has a zeta of around –1.5 to –2.0, so the sample now included companies a little above a B rating. The return to holding these bonds over three years was 73 percent, with a 23.8 percent positive spread over the Blume-Keim index.

Good credit analysis, whether with the Zeta model or some other model, will pay off. Regardless of the credit model, returns should be better with such a model than without.

Defaulted Securities Indices

Up to now, there have been indices to measure performance for all types of equities and fixed-income securities—except defaulted bonds. In the Lipper Analytical Services Fixed-Income Performance booklet, over 30 different types of funds are analyzed, but there is no defaulted bond index. So we built an index for this class starting in 1987. It is now being published in a Merrill Lynch publication, "This is High Yield," as an ongoing measure of defaulted bonds' performance, and is described in detail in Altman and Fridson (1990). The returns obtained in the construction of the index were calculated three different ways (see **Table 8**). The first is a market-weighted index, and the second is an arithmetic average return index.

Since 1987, and through July 1990, investing in every defaulted bond listed in the S&P 500 Bond Guides gave a compound annual rate of return of about 8.6 percent. There is a large degree of variability in the numbers, however, from 38 percent in 1987 to –23 percent in 1989. In the first seven months of 1990, the market-weighted return was –7.0 percent. The arithmetic average was slightly higher than the market-weighted average, a 9 percent return versus the market-weighted return of 8.6 percent.

Table 8. Returns on Defaulted Debt Securities Indices (1987-89)

Period	Average Number of Securities	Annual Return (Market Weighted Average)	Annual Return (Unweighted Average)
1987	61	37.9%	24.0%
1988	89	26.5	20.7
1989	106	–23.0	–16.9
1990 (9 months)	126	–7.0	8.2
1986-89 Arithmetic	96	8.6%	9.0%

Source: "The Altman-Merrill Lynch Defaulted Debt Index." *Extra Credit.* Merrill Lynch & Co. (November 1990)

Finally, **Table 9** shows the correlations between the defaulted debt index and several other indices. It illustrates the diversification potential of investing in defaulted companies' bonds. They would appear to have little systematic risk, because they tend to move more in response to their own situation than with the broader markets. The distressed-debt index has a 50 percent correlation with the S&P 500, 59 percent with the Value Line equity index, and 56 percent with the Merrill Lynch high-yield index. These are relatively low correlation coefficients.

Conclusion

The distressed-securities investor needs to be aware of several things. First, there will be a continued large increase in supply of defaulted debt. Given the laws of supply and demand, even if there is an increase in demand, this large addition to supply is going to put pressure on prices, at least in the short term. Second, there is the problem of liquidity with many of these issues. Investors may not be able to sell the bonds that they want at the prices that they would like. Third, there may be a problem with over-popularity in this area. Of course, this could cause prices to rise in the short term, but it will also cause problems in the long term. The final caveat is that this new "market" is not appropriate for individual investors or novices.

Table 9. Correlation Matrix between Defaulted Debt Security Returns and Various Equity and High Yield Bond Returns (Monthly Return Observations, 1987-90)

	Defaulted Debt	S&P 500 Equity	Value Line Equity	Merrill-Lynch Master High-Yield
Defaulted Debt	1.00	0.50	0.59	0.56
S&P 500 Equity	0.50	1.00	0.87	0.56
Value Line Equity	0.59	0.87	1.00	0.69
Merrill Lynch (HY)	0.56	0.56	0.69	1.00

Source: "The Altman-Merrill Lynch Defaulted Debt Index." *Extra Credit.* Merrill Lynch & Co. (November 1990)

Question and Answer Session

Question: In an efficient market, should returns on a junk bond portfolio that includes distressed and defaulted securities be equivalent, on a risk-adjusted basis, to the return on a risk-free portfolio of the same duration? In other words, isn't a large excess return evidence that investors are being overcompensated for the risks they are assuming?

Altman: The investor should always be compensated for assuming risk. Of course, the measurement of systematic risk is a particular problem in the debt markets. It is correct to say that, as long as there are no significant inefficiencies over time, the risk-adjusted rates of return will be the same on all securities. There were some inefficiencies in the defaulted debt market. In hindsight, the reason that junk bond returns have plummeted in the past year is that there were tremendous excesses in that industry. The securities are not bad by nature, but companies were paying too much to restructure, and they were using far too much debt.

Question: As you mentioned, a figure of 9 or 10 percent of companies with Z-scores below the critical value is similar to the proportion below the value in 1973 and 1974. However, corporate bond spreads today are much tighter relative to Treasuries on an absolute basis than they were then. Is this an inefficiency in the market?

Altman: The Bbb spread today is about 160 basis points above the Treasury rate, which might be an indication of tight spreads. I would be very unhappy with 150 basis points as a promised return, so I do not think that investors are being adequately compensated for the risk they are incurring. It is interesting to note that the spread between Bbb and B ratings is currently over 600 basis points. There seems to be a lot of potential here for the investor willing to take some risk.

Question: Over time, how are Z-scores distorted by high or rising inflation?

Altman: At the beginning of the 1980s, when the United States and Britain were considering changing from historical-cost to current-cost accounting, I was worried that many models, including my own, might become obsolete. There were some studies done at the time on inflation-adjusted accounting numbers

and their impact on bankruptcy prediction models. As it stands now, however, higher inflation does not make the models less effective. Companies may be able to mask their problems for a little while in an inflationary environment, but I do not think that the inflation itself biases the models.

Question: Does the lack of liquidity in the distressed securities market present any problems to you in your analyses?

Altman: It is not very difficult to estimate the interest-rate risk and default-risk elements in fixed-income pricing. However, one of the great research opportunities today is to estimate the liquidity risk premium. I have attempted to do so by estimating the discount on high-yield bonds resulting from the expected default rate—that is, calculate the break-even between investing in junk bonds and Treasury bonds. My research indicates that the market is anticipating a default rate of around 7 to 9 percent in 1991. But this only adjusts for default risk. So the next question is, how much compensation is required for the additional liquidity risk? The answer depends on what you perceive to be the expected default rate. For instance, if the implied default rate is 10 percent, but you believe that the default rate will be 7 percent, then the other 3 percentage points may be the compensation that investors require for liquidity risk. There have been some attempts to measure liquidity risk, but I am not aware of any really good ones. Another part of the problem is obtaining good pricing information.

Question: Hickman (1958) found that, for the period 1900 to 1944, the highest returns were obtained if bonds were purchased on the day bankruptcy was declared. Your studies show that this may not be the case any longer. Do you have an explanation for why this might have occurred?

Altman: I don't know how his holding period was defined in the calculation of the returns. Also, I don't think that he compared purchase on the date of bankruptcy with purchase one, two, three, or six months afterward. The returns may have been better had the purchase date been changed to six months after. Hradsky and Long (1989) found that six months after bankruptcy was the best time. Certainly, part of the difference might be explained by the fact that the types of companies defaulting today are different than they were then. Part of it might be attributable to the fact that there are more people in the business now than during the period of Hickman's study. With a relatively small number of investors buying and everyone else unloading the bonds, prices could be depressed, only to shoot up when the outlook for the company improves. My guess is that if the returns were measured on a residual basis, rather than on the absolute basis that he used, there would have been negative residual returns in the initial months after the bankruptcy also.

Approaches to Investing in Distressed Securities

Active Approaches

Paul S. Levy
Chairman
Lancer Industries Inc.

An active approach to investing in distressed securities is one in which the principals are committed to playing an active role in the management and direction of a corporation. In connection with this commitment, they usually demand either a majority of the stock of the company or control of the board—or both. In other words, the key to the success of this approach is the ability to influence the affairs of the company on a day-to-day basis.

In this presentation, I will outline appropriate ways of identifying managers and making investments in companies that particularly active players may be pursuing. A distinction will also be made between the active approach and the passive approach described by Shelley Greenhaus.[1]

Assembling Your Team

To pursue the active approach to investing in distressed securities, one must assemble a balanced team of people who have the ability to interact with the financial markets. These people must be able to deal with the bondholders of a troubled company throughout the pre-bankruptcy and bankruptcy process. They must be able to conceive, propose, and implement an exchange offer for securities. In addition, members of the team must have the operational skills needed to run a business on a day-to-day basis. The lead partner cannot be the only one on the team with a significant background in the day-to-day management of companies. The workout process is like the early phases of a leveraged buyout, and everyone must be able to operate in this type of environment.

Regardless of how a workout is viewed, there are myriad kinds of financing required. Indeed, there is

often leverage remaining in an overleveraged company that has now been deleveraged. Banks have become extremely reluctant to extend credit to deal sponsors lacking operational experience, whether the business being purchased is distressed or healthy. This is not meant to be pejorative, but rather descriptive of the real world of distressed-firm workouts. In fact, banks have been much more willing to respond to investors who have the experience to manage a company in today's recessionary environment than to those who do not have the experience.

It is important to analyze the credentials of the group sponsoring a distressed company's reorganization plan before purchasing the bonds. Although the securities may look attractive because someone has a plan to work out the problems of the company, several questions about the group need to be answered first. Will they get the financing required? Will they receive the support of the company's board? Do the current bondholders have sufficient trust in the group to commit to a conversion of their debt into equity? The answers to these questions are very important in determining the attractiveness of the proposed investment.

Due Diligence

Another requirement of the active approach is the need to undertake due diligence. There are many aspects of the due diligence process. For example, in troubled companies many liabilities do not appear in public filings or in private placement memoranda circulated by investment bankers searching for capital infusions. Most investors do not bother to quantify the extent of a hidden liability. Everyone knows of the risks of litigation in the EPA area. Therefore,

---

[1]See Mr. Greenhaus's presentation, pp. 47-48.

my firm never takes over management of a company without first undertaking a complete environmental audit to uncover possible EPA liabilities.

Another facet of due diligence involves assessing the company internally; for example, employee morale, capital expenditures, and relationships with customers and suppliers. It is fairly common for companies *in extremis* to skimp on some of their capital commitments. This is particularly true of companies whose performance has been deteriorating for an extended period of time. In formulating a plan for the business, future capital investment must be spelled out. How much of that amount is going toward investments that should have been made but were instead neglected? These are only some of the off-balance-sheet liabilities that are very real. To do a good job and beat the averages, the analyst must get a handle on them.

Criteria for Investment

Investors in distressed securities must establish explicitly the criteria under which they will invest in the equity of a restructured company. For example, Lancer is only ready to invest new equity in a restructured company if (1) the investment can be done on a friendly basis, and (2) any appropriate restructuring of the balance sheet takes place *simultaneously*. Another example is the proposed investment in Southland by the Japanese. This will only be made by Ito-Yakoda if the bondholders go along with the plan that has been proposed. The Japanese have had a chance to work with management, the chance to work with inside projections, and the opportunity to analyze all of the risks without being caught up in a bondholder battle. Obviously, their investment is subject to the decision of the bondholders, and they have a certain amount of salesmanship and compromise ahead of them to get the deal done. But, the important point is that they are not caught up in it economically. In this kind of situation, it is best not to have money committed to what may prove to be a very unpredictable bankruptcy or pre-bankruptcy proceeding.

It is important for the active investor to get the important variables nailed down before money is invested. When it is not possible to do this, the investor must walk away from the investment. For example, Lancer made an offer for Allegheny International. The bid was fully financed, offering 100 cents on the dollar to subordinated and more senior debt. That is a far cry from what ultimately happened. People who bought the bonds at 60 and saw them rise to 80 thought that the rise from 80 to 100

would be a great ride. However, the bondholders' committee turned down the offer of 100 cents on the dollar because it did not pay enough of their accrued and unpaid interest. Then when we offered to pay some of the accrued and unpaid interest, they balked at our not paying their legal fees. After Lancer decided to walk away from the deal, there was a succession of unsuccessful offerings. Finally, Japonica purchased Allegheny. This was perhaps the fifteenth or sixteenth plan that was proposed for the company. The subordinated debt received about 50 cents in stock—a far cry from our 100 cents cash offer.

The active investor must make sure these important issues are resolved before committing. This is the crux of the active approach. The passive approach is a very different investment discipline.

Implementation of the Active Approach

When pursuing a transaction that is not entirely privately negotiated, the investor should be prepared for more give-and-take to get the deal done. One of the problems in the exchange-offer business today is that, invariably, the bondholders are led by one particular investment advisor. With any recapitalization plan, this advisor always says that the bondholders are not getting enough. Admittedly, this is the game, and they should try to get as much as they can. But too much of the burden is put on the buyers, and these investors need to understand that the companies being restructured are in fact *companies*, not simply money-making investment opportunities. There is a world of difference between looking at a company as a financial opportunity and accepting it as a business enterprise.

Some of the problems alluded to here are indeed real problems. We recently concluded a restructuring for Kane Industries. The investment was conditioned on bondholders agreeing to a compromise on their debt. The deal was done with an incredible 99.9 percent acceptance by the bondholders. In order to invest money, we required two-to-one cash flow coverage of the interest payments. The holders were shown our model and projections for cash flow.

Kane was a company that had spent far too little on capital expenditures for four or five years. This had to be corrected, or the company would start losing customers. The bondholders, however, wanted the money for themselves. They wanted it as debt amortization or interest; they did not want to take the losses on their bonds. The question that has to be put to the bondholders—often rhetorically, because they never respond to it—is, What do you want? The active investor is not going to invest in a company only to make the bondholders whole while overseeing the second failure of the company.

There is a major re-equitization occurring today. WestPoint Pepperell is an example. This was an Aa-rated credit, and, despite its current financial problems, the underlying company remains an Aa-rated credit. Now the bondholders are frustrated because they have been offered equity positions for their debt, even though there was no cash to pay the interest on the debt. The company is still very good. The only stumbling block is a financial transaction in which equity has to be substituted for debt. People will fight over marginal amounts and try to get 5 or 10 percent more, but why is it so bad if these companies are re-equitized? To me it would not be so bad if the noteholders at WestPoint Pepperell be-

came all of the equity. Time will tell.

The bondholders must decide who is going to become the steward of the new company. They must choose the group to come in and revitalize the company, the people who will do what must be done to make the company healthy again.

Conclusion

Major opportunities exist today as the market struggles to re-equitize overleveraged companies. Those who are able to navigate the *workout process* without falling out of the boat stand to profit handsomely. Those who can do that *and* manage these companies on a day-to-day basis will do even better.

Approaches to Investing in Distressed Securities

Passive Approaches

Shelley F. Greenhaus

Unlike active approaches, passive approaches to investing in distressed securities do not involve investors managing the companies in which they invest. Passive investors are "opportunistic." They buy public and private securities that no one else wants—securities out of favor because the company is experiencing financial distress. This type of investing takes place when a company is approaching or has just filed for bankruptcy, or when a major business development occurs which puts the viability of the company in jeopardy. These events cause the price of these companies' debt instruments to drop; they provide the catalyst for an opportunistic investor to start buying.

For the opportunistic investor, investment opportunities arise when more traditional investors sell their holdings of distressed-firm securities in the following circumstances:

(1) high-yield mutual funds that are worried about the loss of current yield,

(2) institutions that do not have the time or desire to participate in a workout,

(3) risk-averse investors who are afraid of the criticism they may face for holding the paper of troubled companies,

(4) banks that own small pieces of syndications, but do not want to spend the time or money to do a workout,

(5) insurance companies that can sell a loan to people at a higher price than what appears on their books, and

(6) trade vendors that prefer to use the cash to reinvest in their businesses rather than speculate on the outcome of a reorganization.

In addition, regulators can pressure investors to sell certain issues. During the past two years, the savings and loan institutions and the insurance companies have been under intense regulatory pressure to upgrade their portfolios.

The major source of distressed-firm securities is in the privately issued debt market. The amount of private debt outstanding today is probably twice the amount of public debt outstanding. This produces tremendous opportunities for the passive investor.

Unlike the active investor, the passive investor does not have access to material, nonpublic information before buying. He relies on information that is publicly filed, information from the bankruptcy court, and hired industry experts in analyzing the risk-reward trade-off in each situation.

Upon receiving nonpublic information, an investor would be restricted and unable to build a full position. Because it takes so much time to build a position in many of these securities, in both the public and private markets, the passive investor, unlike the active investor, does not want to become restricted until the buying is finished. The passive investor, therefore, would only want to be restricted after the buying program is completed. Only after buying is completed will he be willing to join a bondholders' committee for an out-of-court restructuring or an in-court bankruptcy. Furthermore, because it is time consuming to assume an active role in restructuring a distressed firm, the position must be large enough to justify the expense of time and effort. An investment would not be worth several months of work for a position of only $1 to $2 million.

Before purchasing any bond or private claim, a strategy for getting out of this position, otherwise known as an exit strategy, should be determined. The exit strategy could be to force a liquidation, in which case knowledge of the asset values and the capital structure is critical. Or the exit strategy might be an equity-for-debt swap, such as has been done with Southland and Interco. In these cases, reorganization models are critical because they help in the determining the new securities' prices. Equally important is understanding the dynamics of the deal; in other words, being able to judge the likelihood of the deal being successful. Another strategy is to position the company to be sold to a group willing to take an equity position. This option provides liquidity to the passive investor, and the opportunity to run and control a company to the active investor.

My own experience with investing in Wheeling-Pittsburgh Steel illustrates my points. After initial bank debt purchases in 1987, I bought unsecured trade claims during 1988 and 1989. Eventually my position reached a face amount of $145 million, equal to 35 percent of the unsecured creditor class, giving my group veto power over the class. Only after the last strategic purchase was I restricted. The next seven months were devoted to working on a consensual plan to be approved within the following 45 days. At that point, the value added from being restricted was clearly cost-effective. The first plan the debtor proposed offered $0.50 on the dollar. The last plan was $0.71 on the dollar.

Outlook

There are plenty of opportunities to invest in distressed securities without taking an active position. These investments are not without risk, however. Passive investors do not manage the companies that they invest in. They merely own the securities. Therefore, they are vulnerable to the decisions of management. Sometimes mistakes are made, so it is important to maintain a diversified portfolio—one that is diversified by industry, by entity, and often by capital tranche.

The opportunities for investing in distressed-firm securities are no longer restricted to business turnarounds. The overleveraging of the 1980s burdened otherwise healthy businesses with tremendous amounts of debt. Financial restructuring situations are much easier to work out than situations involving both financial and operational distress. The 1990s should be a wonderful time for both active and passive investors. The markets for these types of investment vehicles and the ability to make money in these areas are just beginning to emerge.

Question and Answer Session

Question: How many deals do you consider before getting involved in one?

Levy: We do not keep a precise count, but the number is large. There are a host of reasons that we would pass on a deal, and there are different degrees of intensity with which we examine proposed deals. We probably put a lot of work into 10 to 15 proposals before getting one deal that we would pursue. Of course, we look at a much larger number than that before finding those 10 or 15.

Question: How long does it take to do financial due diligence for a potential investment?

Levy: The first look at the possible balance-sheet restructuring and operational cuts in a proposed financial exchange offer can be done in a short time. This is really not financial due diligence, but if someone calls with an interesting opportunity, we can get back to them within three to five days. The basic financial projection takes two to four days once we get the data. For a public company, published financial reports provide the majority of the data. The first step is to calculate a stabilized cash flow, such as earnings before interest, taxes, depreciation, and amortization (EBITDA).

Typically we assume revenues will be flat. We do not assume that things will improve simply because of our arrival on the scene. To illustrate, when everyone stops buying houses, as is happening today, it is not wise to assume that we would be selling a lot of lumber if we went into a lumber business. These are things that we cannot control. Instead, we try to make money by looking at costs rather than sales.

Once the basic financial projection is complete, we develop various scenarios. Based on our experience and discussions with other people, we get an idea of what the bondholders might accept and whether they are interested in cash or stock. Putting together a couple of scenarios does not take long.

We do not consider ourselves particularly adept at doing real estate, technology, fashion, or multi-unit retail deals. These we decline immediately.

Question: How large is your distressed companies fund? How many deals will it be involved in? What size entities will the fund deal with? What is the required hurdle return?

Levy: The maximum size of the fund has been set at $300 million, although I expect it to be smaller, perhaps $225 to $250 million. We are planning to participate in six to eight deals, which would put the average equity investment in the $35 to $50 million range. The size of the entities depends on the capitalization of the company. They will generally be mid-size companies; this is where we believe the greatest opportunities lie. The high-yield story has really been a middle-market story. Our targets will probably have revenues between $100 million and $500 million. The capitalizations will vary more because of the differing amounts of debt that the companies carry. Our target for a return hurdle is 40 percent, but returns are very uncertain. Obviously, returns are a function of the amount invested, duration of the investment, and market multiples. Returns also depend on exit ability. Today, there are fewer good buyers, so returns can be adversely affected.

Question: Please discuss the merits of investing in both the senior and the subordinated debt of a distressed company, and investing in the equity. What is the merit of spreading your investment across the capital structure versus focusing on a single class?

Greenhaus: I do not believe in investing in the equities of bankrupt or distressed companies. Although I think that the equities have value, it is mostly a nuisance value. Normally, equity does not have the asset backing that we require in our investments. We prefer to go as high in the capital structure as possible so that, on the downside, we would still be paid 100 cents on the dollar. The preferred investment is senior or secured debt. As the bankruptcy progresses and we feel more comfortable with the situation, we will buy securities that are lower in the capital structure, for example subordinated debt. An investor must determine where he is going to get the most bang for his buck. Senior debt that is fully covered may only yield a 16 or 17 percent total return, which may not be attractive. We usually look for a bond that trades around 30 to 40 but has the potential to move into the 50 to 60 range within a reasonable period of time. This has a much better risk-reward trade-off than more senior debt.

Levy: If we were to be buyers of distressed securities for the purpose of acquiring control, we would want the fulcrum security—the security that sits in the capitalization structure below the senior debt that is likely to be serviced and above the debt that looks particularly weak. The Revco 13-1/8 bonds are a good example of a fulcrum security. Those bonds could wind up giving their holders the majority of equity in the company. This approach does not always work, however, as illustrated by Marty Whitman's investment in the debentures of Public Service Company of New Hampshire (PSCNH). Two and a half years ago, the securities below the debentures seemed to be badly impaired. He thought that the debentures would be sufficiently impaired so that he would end up with the bulk of the equity and control of PSCNH. As it turns out, bids materialized and the value of the securities skyrocketed. The good news was that he made a lot of money. The bad news was that his returns were not as good as he expected them to be.

Question: Why not offer cash outright for the assets rather than buying the securities and letting the creditors make the distribution? Wouldn't this approach provide the lowest purchase price for an acquisition?

Levy: There are two parts to the answer. First, there is no problem with offering cash for the assets, thereby buying only part of the company. In fact, that is what we were trying to do in the Allegheny case. Management, however, did not want the company broken up. As it turns out, had we been permitted to proceed with our plan, we would have needed the bankruptcy court's approval to sell an asset (under Section 363). In this case, the sale must be in the best interests of the estate. Because the court has final say, if you make a contract to buy an asset, you do not know what your price will be.

The Edgecomb Steel situation illustrates my point. Although Edgecomb is currently troubled, their steel service business is essentially very good. In 1989, the Blackstone Group severely leveraged Edgecomb, then the bottom fell out of the steel business. In 1990, a large French steel maker, Usinor, offered $105 million for Edgecomb's steel business. Now the Edgecomb bondholders are fighting Blackstone—the equity holders—for the money. Blackstone feels that they should get a large piece of the offer, and the bondholders want to limit their losses. Frankly, this is a very effective strategy by Usinor to separate the resolution of the financial problems from the operations.

In addition, this strategy may be a good way to buy assets cheaply, but there may be problems with competing interests. Problems arise in a restructur-

ing when people compare what they are receiving with what they think other parties are getting. People are as interested in what the other guy is getting as in what they are getting, so an offer for assets where the distribution is unspecified often will not work. Likewise, although it may be good from our perspective to buy the assets and let the other people fight over the cash, if the other parties feel that the purchase price benefits us more than them, then they naturally want more.

There are two ways to bring value to the deal. One is to propose and implement an exchange offer or recapitalization that gets people on board. Bringing people to the bargaining table in a business-like manner and getting them to compromise is easier said than done, but it adds value. The second way to add value is to manage the company well, reduce costs, and improve performance beyond that which the prior management provided. If we can add value in these two areas, then we feel we have a chance to buy businesses at effective prices.

Question: Publicly issued forms of debt command a liquidity premium over privately placed debt. Is this premium currently too high to attract you to public debt relative to private debt?

Greenhaus: The discount of private debt relative to public debt changes over time. Six months ago, public debt was much more attractive than private debt. The private debt market does not respond as quickly as the public market does to changes in the environment. After the bond market crashes in 1987 and 1990, the prices of publicly traded bonds dropped drastically, but the private market did not move at all. In those situations, the purchase of public debt is more favorable than the purchase of private debt. Because the market constantly changes, you must continually reevaluate the types and relative costs of the debt that you are buying.

There are several advantages to buying private debt. First, private debt is usually higher in the capital structure than public debt. And second, private debt can often be purchased more easily, so that obtaining the desired position in an issue can usually be accomplished with one or two purchases. An attempt to buy 30 or 40 percent of a class of public bonds will drive the price up. In order to not move the market as drastically, you may need to buy out the holdings of a bank group or pieces of a syndication. So it is also important to be sensitive to the market and the dynamics of the transaction under consideration.

Question: Should vulture investors—that is, investors who buy securities after they have declined in value—be on the same creditors' committee as the par buyers of the past?

Greenhaus: Absolutely. When a person buys public or private debt, he is buying a contract. The company does not and should not care what price is paid for it. Whether the contract was purchased for par or less than par, the company owes and the holder deserves all the rights and privileges that the contract specifies. The vulture investor deserves the same amount of money that anyone else would receive. A lot of people believe that vulture investors take advantage of the lack of information and are not productive. A lot of the par buyers are intransigent and carry a lot of animosity toward management. Because the vultures go into the situation looking for an economic return, they often force the process to move along much quicker than if they had not been involved.

Levy: I agree with that idea. If someone has a trade claim and wants to sell it, that is his business. The transfer of ownership does not diminish the size of the claim against the company. When vulture investors invest in a troubled situation, securities are moved into the hands of people who understand the process and who are prepared to make a deal.

Question: Do opportunities for investing in distressed companies extend to international markets?

Levy: Yes, although there are differences between the U.S. market and international markets for distressed securities. We have been inundated lately by London companies and investment banks that focus on distressed securities. There are a lot of companies in England that are going bad. For instance, there is Parkfield in the steel forgings business, and there is Colorall, which is in textiles. In England, absolute priority is the rule. They do not have a concept of rehabilitation, which is the Chapter 11 process. In England, one of the well-known public accounting firms is appointed as receiver. The receiver takes control of the businesses and sells them off. Whatever proceeds are generated are paid out in order of priority. That is the entire story. There is talk of instituting a rehabilitative process similar to Chapter 11, but that has not yet happened. Rehabilitation does not exist in France either, and in Germany it is not uncommon for officers of bankrupt companies to be jailed.

Greenhaus: The fact that the solutions are different opens up a lot of opportunities. We were recently

involved with Bond Brewing, which is an Australian company controlled by Alan Bond. We purchased a large position of their U.S.-denominated bonds and earned some very handsome returns. Australia has laws very similar to those in England, so that if a company cannot pay its debts, the businesses are liquidated and debt is paid down on an absolute-priority basis. As long as you are comfortable investing on asset value, you can make a tremendous amount of money.

Levy: I wonder when the rule of absolute priority will reassert itself in the American workout community. I remember a case in which a holder of subordinated debt believed that the senior debt should not get more than 5 percent above what he received. He said that the difference in interest rate was only 50 or 75 basis points, so the difference in recovery shouldn't be as large as it was. So I asked him why his bonds said "subordinated" and the other bonds said "senior subordinated." People do not think in terms of absolute priority. Because there are so many consensual plans in America, people have been lulled into believing that plans should be consensual. Non-consensual plans, or cram-downs, are not often used here.

Question: Would you advise holders of distressed credits to make their own new equity investments for their debt obligations during the restructuring process? Or should they use an outside source, such as Lancer, as their equity investor?

Greenhaus: For most corporations that have made a bad investment, it would not be possible for the workout officer to convince the board to commit more money. It may make sense financially and intellectually to put another $10 million into a corporation, while holding $20 million of distressed notes, but the officer could never sell the idea to the board. Also, even if the deal is economically correct, it would be very difficult to get agreement of a majority of the bondholder group to proceed with the deal. Most bondholders do not want to own the equity. They like bonds and bond-like instruments. Maybe the equity is worth a lot, but bondholders are much more comfortable having a bond instrument that they understand. It is tremendously difficult in a bankruptcy to move from the bond side to the equity side.

Levy: Bondholders are not prepared to make those investments. Some bondholders have threatened action, but most do not because they are not as good as an outsider in making equity investments. If banks would participate in restructuring programs as lenders they could make more money from asset recovery than they do from many of their other endeavors. The banks would not even have to commit new money, but would just need to take some losses on current debt and push the deficiency into equity holdings. American banks would wind up with significant equity positions, like Deutsche Bank in Germany. This is a significant area of missed opportunity. The difficulty is that there is an institutional bias against admitting to problem loans. It's a shame because they are the ones who are best positioned to take advantage of these opportunities.

Murray: This is clearly one of the reasons that this market has characteristics of inefficiency. The lenders know the enterprise inside and out. Because they are presumably over the hurdle of getting acquainted with the company, they should be able to participate in the provision of equity as part of the restructuring. People will not generally bring to the directors' committee an opportunity to invest in a company that has caused them losses and write-downs.

Question: How has the LTV decision affected distressed-exchange issues, and what ramifications will it have in the future?

Greenhaus: In the short term, it has made exchange offers more difficult. I believe that there will be more bankruptcies because of this. In the longer term, indentures and exchange offers will be restructured to deal with some of the problems caused by these decisions. It's all part of the constant evolution of the bankruptcy code and the bankruptcy process.

Levy: I don't think it will have any ramifications. The only danger from the LTV decision is one of relativity. If there is a subsequent problem, the people who did not participate in the initial restructuring should not wind up in a dramatically better position than those who did participate, assuming both received debt. This problem is solved, in effect, by having fewer holdouts. LTV should not cause problems if the acceptance levels are at the requisite level.

Evaluating Distressed Securities: A Case Study

Jeffrey I. Werbalowsky
Managing Director, Financial Restructuring Group
Houlihan, Lokey, Howard & Zukin Capital

Financial distress, a company's inability to service obligations arising from its capital structure, differs from operational distress, a company's inability to function in the market in an acceptable manner. A distressed firm may exhibit both forms of distress in different measure. In this presentation, I will offer an analytical framework for valuing the securities of a company undergoing financial distress.

Analysis of a distressed situation is often colored by the strong emotions of the participants in rationalizing their respective entitlement to some increased recovery relative to other claimants. This zero-sum mentality—that is, for every gain, there is a loss—is not always valid in distressed situations. Often, a collective solution to a distressed situation is possible. Ideally, restructuring benefits can be allocated among the constituencies through a positive-sum game in which all constituencies can maintain or improve their recoveries. A key element in reaching a consensual restructuring is to illustrate this dynamic to the various parties. Sophisticated, recurrent participants (such as certain funds and financial institutions and their advisors) in restructuring transactions pay more than lip service to this concept, as evidenced by the plethora of out-of-court workouts in progress today.

The Analytical Framework

When a company cannot satisfy the terms of its debt, it must assess and modify its capital structure. To embark on such a course, some general game plan is needed. I generally employ some variant of the following steps:

Identify the problem. Is the firm in financial distress, operational distress, or both? The term "financial distress" describes a company that generates a reasonable level of cash flow but has promised to pay out too much of its cash flow in fixed payments, usually debt payments—in other words, it is over-leveraged. "Operational distress" describes a company that cannot generate an appropriate level of cash flow—for example, a company faced with a business problem arising from inadequate revenue generation or overwhelming costs.

Financial engineering can work if applied correctly to situations of financial distress, but it does not cure operational distress. The goal of a financial restructuring is to create a stable and viable company that can generate the cash flow necessary to satisfy all claimants and shareholders over the long term. The most brilliant restructuring techniques will not work if the company continues to lose money on an operational basis. If the problem is operational distress, then the company needs turn-around managers and people to reassess the business. It may need to liquidate parts of the business. A company exhibiting operational distress cannot be rationally restructured without first addressing this problem.

Calculate the value of the company. This is a basic consideration in every restructuring transaction. The methodologies used most often to determine value are the discounted cash flow, market comparables, and liquidation approaches. Various modifications to these familiar analyses are often necessary. EBIT (earnings before interest and taxes) multiples cannot be used if the EBIT is not representative of the company's future prospects (for example, if EBIT is zero or negative). Valuation of tax attributes, such as net operating losses, can be quite complex. A brief description of these valuation issues follows.

Calculate the value of each element of the capital structure. Although not an easy task, it is necessary to determine the present distressed worth of each component of the capital structure. This task is complicated because the absolute priority rule does not apply in the real world, except in the most unusual and exigent circumstances, such as a foreclosure or Chapter 7 liquidation. Bondholders are technically, but not practically, "entitled" to the residual value of a distressed firm after secured debt is paid. In a severely distressed situation, however, secured debtholders may not even be in a practical position to recover the value of the collateral they bargained for. The practical valuation of a class of debt or equity is necessary to allow the holders of that class the opportunity to evaluate a modification of their rights, and value, in a restructuring transaction.

The enforceability of contractual relationships—what bond indentures and security agreements say—is an important guide to negotiation and resolution of allocation issues, but rarely is it dispositive. After three years of a bankruptcy and the judge getting tired of the company being in Chapter 11, you may eventually get an absolute priority distribution, but you cannot count on that. Deviation from absolute priority and restructuring transactions, in and out of bankruptcy, is needed to value companies, securities, and investment opportunities accurately. Such deviations reflect the settlement dynamic of senior claimants being pressured into accepting less by the equity.

The process of evaluating distressed companies and their securities includes the following steps:

1. *Start with equity.* The first thing to understand in valuing distressed situations is that equity is never worth zero. The control value, option value, and nuisance value of equity are zero. Almost every distressed analysis I have read starts with the highest priority claims usually leading to an omission or underestimation of equity value. Assessing equity value avoids this analytical error.

2. *Value the secured debt and bank debt.* Bank debt may be totally secured, but it is often not "worth" 100 cents on the dollar. The financial element of distress is only one consideration in the valuation of distressed situations. Legal considerations, particularly bankruptcy law, are very important. In fact, the greater the degree of distress, the greater the importance of legal analysis in accurately valuing distressed securities. Even in an out-of-court restructuring, rational people compare the results to what they can get in bankruptcy proceedings. If you do not know what you can get in bankruptcy, how can you know what to settle for out of court? Similarly, if you are in a bankruptcy situation, is your debt vulnerable to a "cram down?" Can it be equitably subordinated? Did you buy from someone who has perpetuated a fraudulent conveyance? You do not have to be a lawyer, but you must understand that factors beyond the financial elements are at work to determine value in distressed transactions. This can be of particular importance in valuing seemingly fully secured claims, as a number of banks have discovered over the years.

3. *Value the "intermediate" elements of the capital structure.* Between the collateral-related value of secured debt and the control-related value of equity lies the universe of unsecured claims and preferred stock. Whether one is valuing simple trade debt or the most complex subordinated debenture, value is a function of both the residual value of the enterprise allocable to the class of claims or interests and the legal rights accorded that constituency. These classes are neither "fish nor fowl," with seniority above the controlling party equity, but without the powerful rights to collateral enjoyed by secured creditors. Obviously, valuation in each instance is a question of particular facts, as discussed later.

4. *Determine an optimal capital structure for the firm.* In almost every deal I have been involved in, substantial deleveraging makes sense, but it is rarely applied. A continual phenomenon in restructuring transactions is that companies come out over-leveraged because people prefer debt over equity. Institutions do not like equity because they cannot value it or "book" it like debt. A million other reasons explain this preference, but unfortunately, all of them often make the restructuring process a perpetuation of financial distress rather than a resolution.

The parties should start with a capital structure that makes sense for the restructured company. This is achieved through conservative projection of future cash flows and needs, as well as an understanding of the relative financial condition of competitors. Moreover, the tax position of the company (as well as the restructuring participants) must be understood. If the restructured company maintains substantial net operating losses, for example, and all claimants are corporations, preferred stock (because of the corporate dividend exclusion) might make sense as a material component of the new capital structure.

5. *Negotiate an allocation of the value of the restructured enterprise.* In every successful restructuring transaction, the value of a restructured enterprise is greater than its value prior to the restructuring. For example, resolution of financial distress often leads to at least a partial restoration of trade credit, improvement in employee attitude, redeployment of top management's attention, and improved perception among customers. All of those things, which are very difficult to quantify, can add to enterprise value. There is empirical evidence of this in the increased aggregate prices of stocks and bonds of a distressed company when a plan of reorganization is proposed or confirmed or when an exchange offer is consummated. Deciding how these benefits are to be divided among the banks, bondholders, trade creditors, and equity holders usually occupies a great deal of time and effort in the restructuring process.

6. *Determine how to implement the restructuring plan.* Should there be an out-of-court exchange offer? If so, what type of a securities law approach should be utilized? Do we simply talk to the banks and ask them to be reasonable? Do we just go down to the bankruptcy court and file? Do we try to do a pre-packaged Chapter 11? All of these options have their advantages and disadvantages, which must be weighed in the context of determining how best to meet the goals of a successful restructuring. Particular consideration needs to be given to the pros and cons of the bankruptcy process. **Exhibit 1** summarizes the major similarities and differences between an exchange offer and the bankruptcy process.

Valuation of Individual Securities

Valuation of the individual securities of a distressed company is an interactive process requiring analysis of the particular bargaining strengths of each creditor and equity class. The uncertainties, risks, and expenses of the restructuring process may seriously impair enterprise value, but the resolution of financial distress and the elimination of these burdens have a positive effect on value. The allocation of these risks, burdens, and benefits may have a substantial impact on securities value. Some of these issues can be illustrated with an example.

Xcorp: A Case Study

Some of these restructuring issues will be illustrated using the case of Xcorp, a fictional corporation that underwent a leveraged buyout on January 1, 1987. Xcorp, a manufacturer and retailer of various apparel products, is capitalized with senior secured bank debt, one class of subordinated debt, trade debt, preferred stock, and common stock. Xcorp "hit the wall" in late 1989, and we evaluate Xcorp's situation as of this date. I note that the valuation analysis performed as of late 1989 already seems unrealistically optimistic today, in late 1990.

Xcorp has three stand-alone divisions: Bigco, Cashco, and Sickco. A more usual corporate structure would include subsidiaries, but to simplify the tax and securities issues, all assets of Xcorp are held by one corporate entity.

Bigco is a solid division that manufactures consumer and intermediate products, primarily apparel fabrics for the sportswear market and branded sportswear and footwear products. It is a major player in a mature industry. Its success largely

---

Exhibit 1. Comparison of Exchange Offer and Bankruptcy Process

Selected similarities between bankruptcy and exchange offer processes:

- Classification and treatment of debt and equity classes
- Seek optimal capital structure
- Structure securities within parameters of cash flow
- Allocate restructuring values based on fair market value of class holdings
- Awareness of NOL preservation and utilization
- Limited exemption from securities regulation

Selected differences between bankruptcy and exchange offer processes:

- Bankruptcy Code (Section 1125 disclosure, Section 1129 general confirmation requirements) establishes transaction parameters, rather than securities laws
- Disparity in tax treatment; I.R.C. Sections 108 and 382
- Variety of extraordinary powers and privileges in Chapter 11, including:
  . Automatic stay under Section 362
  . Asset sales "free and clear" under Section 363
  . Rejection of executory contracts under Sections 365 and 1113
  . Recovery of avoidable transfers under Section 544 *et seq.*
  . Limitation on interest accrual on unsecured and undersecured debt under Section 502(b)(2)
  . Ability to cure and reinstate contracts and claims under Sections 365 and 1126
  . Cram down of secured debt under Section 1129(b)(2)(A)
- Can bind minority holdouts within a creditor or interest class, subject to Section 1126 acceptance provisions and Section 1129(a)(7) best interests test
- Can bind class holdouts through cram down subject to, *inter alia*, Section 1129(b)(2)(B-C) compliance

Source: Werbalowsky and Stanford (1989).

depends on just-in-time inventory management and short manufacturing lead times. It is a major supplier to Cashco. It is not an exciting company, but it is a cash cow. It has been around for 34 years.

Cashco is a retailer in a specialty niche. It operates sports fitness centers in the southwestern and central United States, retailing athletic footwear and accessories. Sales growth has been high because of store openings. Moderate to low capital expenditures are needed, store leases are acquired from existing mom-and-pop operators, and stores are modified to uniform style and quality. Cashco's growth rate has been good during the past five years, and it has generated substantial cash while growing. It is the most-value-per-revenue-dollar aspect of Xcorp's three divisions.

Sickco is a manufacturer of specialty intermediate products. It manufactures unique outerwear fabric with enhanced water resistance, insulation, and breathability features. It is a minor supplier to Bigco. The division is not doing well. Competition, product development, and manufacturing problems have hurt sales and margins. It has potential—it is working on something that will make Gortex look like denim; however, every month the key engineers keep saying "maybe next month." They have not been able to perfect this critical product, so rather than doing better, Sickco continues to do poorly. At the time of the LBO, everyone was assured that Sickco would turn around and break even within one year. Its bleed rate has accelerated since then.

Xcorp was purchased for $280 million plus assumption of current liabilities in a management-sponsored buyout. **Table 1** shows the sources and uses of funds in the transaction. The post-LBO capital structure is composed of $150 million in eight-year term loans from a syndicate of eight banks at prime plus 2 percent; $100 million in 14-percent subordinated debentures due in 1999; 2 million shares of $10-per-share liquidation preference, 11.5 percent dividend cumulative preferred stock; and 10 million

Table 1. LBO Transaction of Xcorp in 1987 ($ in millions)

Sources:	$150	Secured loan
	100	Subordinated debt
	20	Preferred stock
	10	Common stock
	$280	Total sources
Uses:	$ 80	Repayment of existing debt
	190	Purchase of existing common stock
	10	Payment of transaction fees
	$280	Total uses

Source: Werbalowsky and Stanford (1989).

shares of no-par-value common stock.

Table 2 presents Xcorp's pre- and post-transaction balance sheet. Using an IRC Section 338 election, Xcorp "wrote up" its purchased assets using purchase accounting and assigned $16 million of purchase price to unidentified intangible assets (goodwill) and $10 million of transaction fees to other assets. This allowed Xcorp substantial depreciation deductions. Coupled with the interest from the deal debt, these deductions provided a great tax shield. Because earnings have fallen far short of projections, this has resulted in a build-up of net operating loss carryforwards.

Table 2. Xcorp Balance Sheet ($ in millions)

Pre-Transaction				
Current assets	$ 70		Current liabilities	$ 22
Fixed assets	100		Secured loan	80
			Total liabilities	102
			Common stock	68
Total assets	$170		Total liabilities and stockholders' equity	$170
Post-Transaction				
Current assets	$ 66		Current liabilities	$ 22
Fixed assets	210		Secured loan	150
Goodwill	16		Subordinated debt	100
Other assets	10		Total liabilities	272
			Preferred stock	20
			Common stock	10
Total assets	$302		Total liabilities and stockholders' equity	$302

Source: Werbalowsky and Stanford (1989).

Management paid hefty multiples by today's standards to acquire the company. **Table 3** presents several measures of what management paid for the company. The multiples are based on 1986 EBIT of $28.1 million. Depreciation and amortization was $8.2 million; earnings before depreciation, interest, and taxes (EBDIT) was $36.3 million.

Shortly after Xcorp's LBO, some alarming elements began to appear. First, interest rates began to rise, increasing interest expense on Xcorp's floating-rate secured debt. Profitability declined somewhat at Bigco, and losses have risen at Sickco (while Cashco has "held its own"). Bigco has required substantial additional unbudgeted capital expenditures to maintain its market position. Lengthening of trade payables (part of the LBO plan) has damaged Xcorp's excellent credit reputation and reduced Xcorp's access to trade credit.

In distressed situations, management has few

Table 3. LBO Implied Transaction Multiples ($ in millions)

Method	Price		Level	=	Implied Multiple
Earnings before interest and taxes (EBIT)	$280.0	÷	$28.1	=	10.0
Earnings before depreciation, interest, and taxes (EBDIT or EBITD)	$280.0	÷	$36.3	=	7.7
Debt-free earnings (DFE)	$280.0	÷	$16.9	=	16.6
Debt-free cash flow (DFCF)	$280.0	÷	$25.1	=	11.2

Source: Werbalowsky and Stanford (1989).

options for raising cash: they cannot borrow more from the bank, they cannot go back to the bond-holders, and the equityholders will not kick in more money. One option is to rely heavily on involuntary lenders—the trade creditors—and Xcorp has increasingly attempted to tap this desperate source of funds.

Xcorp in Financial Distress

As of July 1989, Xcorp is in technical default on its senior loan covenants and projects that it will have insufficient cash to meet $12 million of payments on its bank and bond debt due in two months. Xcorp's earnings and cash flow levels have been disappointingly below management's projections. The relatively small discrepancies from projections, as shown in **Table 4**, created severe and substantial financial distress. Although these numbers are not so bad, they are enough to put Xcorp in severe financial distress. The overleveraging of Xcorp has resulted in a financial structure that can stand no deviation from perfection, especially where deal multiples have fallen

and financing sources are restricted.

In distressed situations, people want to find something that will save the company. This might be an investor, a great sale of a troubled division, or a merger. At the last minute, it inevitably falls through. For Xcorp, a foreign financial player has offered $18 million for Sickco. Although no rational person would buy Sickco for $18 million, Xcorp management wants to believe and devotes substantial effort to closing the deal. In reality, even an $18 million sale of Sickco will not solve the problem, because the bank will want all the money and Xcorp still has to make the subordinated debt payments. Moreover, the cash flow-generating ability of the rest of the company is never going to be sufficient to satisfy the debt. The company is now coming face to face with the fact that it needs to restructure, especially when (surprise!) the Sickco sale falls through.

Analysis of the Situation

Xcorp's capital structure is no longer viable. The

Table 4. Five-Year Divisional Financial Summary—1987 Plan Projections Versus Actual ($ in millions)

	Pre-Transaction		Post-Transaction		
Sales	*1985*	*1986*	*1987*	*1988*	*1989**
Actual					
Bigco	$220.0	$228.4	$237.0	$246.3	$251.2
Cashco	59.0	64.3	69.4	75.0	78.4
Sickco	38.0	41.0	43.1	45.2	47.4
Consolidated	$317.0	$333.7	$349.5	$366.5	$377.0
Plan	N/A	N/A	350.0	379.0	405.0
EBDIT					
Actual					
Bigco	$ 23.5	$ 24.6	$ 25.6	$ 26.3	$ 26.4
Cashco	6.8	7.7	8.0	8.7	9.1
Sickco	3.8	4.0	4.1	2.3	(1.0)
Consolidated	$ 34.1	$ 36.3	$ 37.7	$ 37.3	$34.5
Plan	N/A	N/A	$ 39.6	$ 43.1	$ 47.0
EBDIT/Sales (%)					
Actual					
Bigco	10.7	10.7	10.8	10.7	10.5
Cashco	11.5	12.0	11.5	11.6	11.6
Sickco	10.0	10.0	9.5	5.0	(2.0)
Consolidated	10.8	10.9	10.8	10.2	9.2
Plan	N/A	N/A	11.3	11.5	11.6

* Estimated

Source: Werbalowsky and Stanford (1989).

company cannot be expected to meet its upcoming principal and interest payments or to provide sufficient funds to satisfy Xcorp's critical needs for refurbishment and replacement of plant and equipment. In valuing the securities of Xcorp and determining a restructuring plan, consideration must be given to its imminent payment default and the methods available to it in attempting to resolve its financial distress.

Xcorp can pursue one or more paths to develop liquidity, including the following:

- *Sell assets.* This works if you sell low cash-generating assets, but selling high cash-generating assets for a fair price may postpone, but does not generally solve, an overleverage problem. The only way selling assets works in a highly leveraged situation is if you sell for a good price assets that are not generating a relatively large cash flow.

- *Informally seek modification of bank debt, subordinated debt, or trade debt.* Informally seeking modifications of your subordinated debt is difficult. You generally need to go through some kind of formal exchange offer or consent solicitation. In the case of Xcorp, bondholders have formed an informal committee and hired legal and financial advisors to negotiate on their behalf.

- *Convince Xcorp's banks to advance additional funds.* In a smaller situation, if you had a good relationship with a bank lending officer and you could show the bank a way out of the problem, getting additional funds has been possible (in the past, at least). Even in larger situations, banks have "stepped up to the plate" if a viable plan has been presented. That is an increasingly rare occurrence today.

- *Convince the LBO sponsor or management to invest additional capital.* Usually this is done in connection with the restructuring, because most funds will not throw good money after bad without curing the capital structure problem.

- *Locate a source of new capital.* All kinds of vulture investors are looking for a good company with a bad debt structure. The problem is, they are trying to create rates of return that are substantial, and those rates of return come at the expense of bondholders or other residual claimants. As a side note, many "vulture investors" are finding it easier to locate situations in which the securities are undervalued than situations in which an investor can make a good return by financing a major restructuring without bringing some sort of operational synergy. In many cases, creditors want to get out of a bad situation, but

not at the substantial discounts necessary to give financial buyers of distressed situations the windfall they are looking for.

- *Structure a formal exchange offer.* There are a lot of legal ramifications to the maze of exchange offer options. Tender offers, consent solicitations, indenture modifications, and 3(a)(9), 4(2), and even 3(a)(10) exchange offers can be considered. It is important to understand the securities law and financial implications behind all these techniques.

- *Solicit acceptances for a "pre-packaged" Chapter 11 plan.* Section 1126(b) of the Bankruptcy Code enables a company to effect a "quick" bankruptcy by soliciting consents to a plan of reorganization outside bankruptcy. It then files a Chapter 11 case and immediately confirms the accepted plan and binds holdouts—a pure exchange offer. Exchange offers, in which 80 or 90 percent of the creditors must agree to the plan, are hard to complete in many situations. Everyone has a collective incentive in restructuring transactions to make sure that everyone tenders, but everyone also has an individual incentive to hold out because the more bonds tendered into a situation, the further the company deleverages, and the higher the value of the holdout bonds. In other words, the company cannot make payments on $100 million of junk debt bearing 15 percent interest. If 90 percent of the junk debt converts to equity, however, the company can pay the 15 percent interest on the 10 percent of the junk debt left outstanding. Of the many advantages of a prepackaged Chapter 11, the greatest is that it cures the holdout problem if at least two-thirds in amount and over one-half in number voting accept the plan. In these situations, *all* creditors in the accepting class, including holdouts, are bound to the treatment in the plan.

- *File for protection under Chapter 11 of the Bankruptcy Code.* In many distressed situations, companies have unsuccessfully attempted one or more of the above solutions and are faced with foreclosure or other imminent financial disaster. For them, Chapter 11 is the last option.

Many of these options are not feasible for Xcorp. Its attempted sale of Sickco to an industry competitor already fell through. Sale of other divisions is not immediately feasible. Talks with Xcorp's banks have not obtained unilateral concessions—banks are willing to negotiate only in the context of an exchange offer involving the subordinated debt. The banks will not advance additional funds. Neither the LBO sponsor nor management are prepared to invest additional funds. Xcorp decides that the disruptions and costs of bankruptcy may possibly be avoided by first attempting an out-of-court solution through an exchange offer. Many major distressed transactions, especially busted LBOs, try out-of-court workouts and exchange offers. If they fail, then they go into bankruptcy. When distress is catastrophic—something that comes on all of a sudden—there is no point in starting with an exchange offer, because it cannot help. These firms go straight into Chapter 11; the company needs the bankruptcy process for reasons beyond just the restructuring of funded debt. Examples of cases in which a bankruptcy was "necessary" are Texaco, Smith International, Siliconix (all litigation "disasters"), Johns Manville, A.H. Robbins (mass tort claims), and Continental I (rejection of labor agreement).

After reviewing the options, Xcorp announces that it will pursue the renegotiation of its senior and subordinated debt through bank discussions and a Section 4(2) exchange offer.

Valuation of Xcorp

The first step is to value Xcorp—that is, determine the size of the pie to be divided. The enterprise value of Xcorp will be estimated using two approaches: the discounted cash flow (DCF) approach, and the market-comparable approach.

The Discounted Cash Flow Model

Using the DCF model, the value of the company is equal to the present value of its debt-free cash flows plus the present value of its terminal value, which in this case is determined as of 1995. The terminal value is calculated using a perpetuity valuation approach. The key variables used in the perpetuity valuation approaches are the growth rate assumed for the company's cash flows going forward, and the discount rate. In this case, the positive impact of Xcorp's net operating losses on cash flows and value also must be considered.

The discount rate used is a weighted-average cost of capital (WACC), determined for enterprise valuations using an appropriate capital structure for

a competitor within Xcorp's industry (or Xcorp's expected capital structure after the workout is completed). In distressed situations, the company's future cash flows are more variable (risky) than those of comparable companies. The reasons include a short-term crisis-management perspective and a higher probability of near-bankruptcy costs arising from inadequate working capital-related problems, professional fees, an inability to implement long-range plans, an inability to attract and retain valuable employees, an instability of contractual relationships, and human disruption.

A review of Xcorp's industry indicates a normal capital structure is composed of approximately 65 percent debt and 35 percent equity. Using the Capital Asset Pricing Model, the cost of equity is determined to be 20 percent. The average cost of debt is 14.25 percent. The average tax rate is assumed to be zero for purposes of the exchange offer, because the company is expected to offset any positive taxable income with net operating losses during the next five years. Thus, the tax shield traditionally provided by debt is inoperative. Using these data, the WACC is 16.25 percent [(14.25% × 0.65) + (20% × 0.35)].

Table 5 presents the projected cash flows for Xcorp for the five-year valuation period. The forecast is based on the following assumptions. Annual sales growth is 7 percent for Cashco, 5 percent for Bigco, and 3.9 percent for Sickco. Divisional profitability remains constant, except for Sickco, which achieves break-even profitability by 1990 and a return to fiscal 1987 profit levels by 1994. Consolidated gross margins increase as higher-margin Cashco sales become a larger component of total sales. Capital expenditures increase slightly, but not enough to meet actual Bigco requirements.

Table 6 contains a matrix of Xcorp's present discounted value for a range of WACCs and terminal values, where terminal values vary because of differing growth assumptions. The range reflects uncertainty with respect to the company's "normal" capital structure and riskiness of cash flows. The range of values provides information on the sensitivity of

Table 5. Projected Cash Flow of Xcorp ($ in millions)

	1990	1991	1992	1993	1994
Projected revenues, net	$391.196	$411.425	$432.750	$455.750	$478.945
EBIT	19.475	22.199	25.609	29.783	34.490
Taxes (40%)	(7.790)	(8.880)	(10.244)	(11.913)	(13.796)
DFE	11.685	13.319	15.366	17.870	20.694
Capital expenditures	(5.000)	(5.000)	(5.000)	(5.000)	(6.000)
Depreciation and amortization	15.666	15.998	16.264	16.529	16.795
Change in W/C	(6.449)	(0.467)	(2.675)	(2.687)	(2.861)
DFCF	$ 15.902	$ 23.850	$ 24.955	$ 27.712	$ 30.628

Source: Werbalowsky and Stanford (1989).

Table 6. Present Value of Xcorp's Five-Year Interim Cash Flows and Terminal Value in Year Five ($ in millions)

Present Value of Interim Flows and Terminal Value

		Annual Growth Rates		
	WACC	3.00%	4.00%	5.00%
	15.00%	199	212	227
Discount	15.50%	191	202	215
Rates	16.00%	183	193	205
	16.50%	176	185	196[1]

Implied 1990 EBDIT Multiple

		Annual Growth Rates		
	WACC	4.00%	5.00%	6.00%
	15.00%	5.7	6.0	6.4
Discount	15.50%	5.4	5.8	6.1
Rates	16.00%	5.2	5.5	5.8
	16.50%	5.0	5.3	5.6

(1) The average value represented in the boxed area is 195 million, which represents an average EBDIT multiple of 5.5.

Source: Werbalowsky and Stanford (1989).

the terminal value to different growth rates. Historically, Xcorp's sales growth exceeded inflation by 2 to 3 percent. Thus, assuming inflation rates of 3 to 4 percent, the 4 to 5 percent terminal annual growth rate assumptions appear reasonable (even though perpetual "real growth cannot be sustained).

Given a range of terminal growth rates of 4 to 5 percent, and the 15.5-percent and 16.5-percent WACCs, the values range from $185 million to $215 million. Interpolating between the four numbers, the value of Xcorp is estimated to be $195 million. This yields an implied (future) 1990 EBDIT multiple of 5.5 ($195 ÷ $35.141 = 5.5).

Market-Comparable Valuation Approach

The values of publicly traded companies that are in similar lines of business to Xcorp can also be used to value Xcorp. Because we are valuing the operating assets of a company, the simplifying assumption is often made that the value of the publicly traded company's operating assets is equal to its interest-bearing debt, preferred stock liquidation value, and its common stock on a controlling-interest basis. Because observed stock prices reflect minority-owned interests in a company, an appropriate control premium must be selected. Based upon an analysis of acquisitions of publicly traded companies in businesses similar to Xcorp, a control premium of 25 percent is selected. The estimates must be adjusted for qualitative factors, such as net operating loss (NOL)-utilization potential and the quality of earnings. If your comparables have NOLs, however, then their multiples already take into account the fact that those companies can shield future income. Additionally, the comparables may possess substantial nonoperating assets such as excess cash, undeveloped real estate, and investment portfolios. These are taken into account as well.

The next step is to calculate how much the market value capitalizes the comparable company's debt-free earnings and cash flows. The result is a calculation of market valuation multiples. **Table 7** shows the market valuation multiples of five similar companies, using four calculations of the multiples.

Although the comparable companies may be similar to Xcorp, they do not possess identical risks and opportunities. An investment risk analysis is used to quantitatively and qualitatively compare Xcorp to each comparable company from an investment-risk perspective. Xcorp is a greater investment risk than the comparable public companies and is most similar to, but weaker than, Mendocino Manufacturing. In this type of situation, it is advisable to select valuation multiples at or below the low end of the range for public companies. **Table 8** presents the range of values using the market valuation approach. The high value is $195 million and the low

Table 7. Market Valuation Multiples (Control Premium = 35 Percent)

	Price/EBIT	Price/EBDIT	Price/DFE	Price/DFCF
Sacramento & Sons	14.3	8.1	16.7	9.1
Orange Associates	12.3	8.3	18.9	10.8
Mendocino Manufacturing	15.4	7.7	25.6	9.6
Angeles Amalgamated	12.8	8.3	21.3	11.2
Diego Diversified	12.7	6.8	21.1	8.7
High	15.4	8.3	25.6	11.2
Low	12.3	6.8	16.7	8.7
Median	12.8	8.1	21.1	9.6
Selected	11.0	6.0	18.5	7.5
% of Median	85.9%	75.0%	87.7%	78.1%

Source: Werbalowsky and Stanford (1989).

Table 8. Market Comparable Valuation of Xcorp ($ in millions)

	Projected 1989 Xcorp Level	Selected Multiple	Value Indication
Price/EBIT	$17.2	11.0	$189.2
Price/EBDIT	32.5	6.0	195.0
Price/DFE	10.3	18.5	190.6
Price/DFCF	25.6	7.5	192.0
Median			193.5
Selected			195.0

Source: Werbalowsky and Stanford (1989).

value is $189.2 million. This is similar to the valuations derived using the DCF approach.

Other Considerations

In the Xcorp example, the company has more than $60 million in NOLs based upon hypothetical post-restructuring capital structure. I conclude that the value of the NOL is approximately $5.0 million. Xcorp currently suffers from a working capital deficit equal to $5.0 million, however. These two elements offset, so no adjustment is made to total value.

Valuation of Xcorp with Enhanced Capital Structure

The value of Xcorp with an enhanced capital structure must be calculated. With an improved (but not optimal) capital structure, Xcorp's earnings and cash flows should be valued closer to the median of the range of public comparables, all other things being equal. The potential value of Xcorp with an enhanced, deleveraged capital structure is presented in **Table 9**. The values range from $217.3 million to $263.3 million.

Based on the WACC declining 150 basis points to 15 percent to reflect the reduced risk, and assuming a 4-percent to 5-percent terminal growth rate, the discounted cash flow approach yields a range of values from $212 million to $227 million.

Several qualitative issues should be addressed in confirming a post-restructuring value. First, a successful exchange offer will remove the cloud of un-

Table 9. Market Comparable Valuation of Xcorp with Enhanced Capital Structure ($ in millions)

Method	Projected 1989 Xcorp Level	Median Multiple	Value
EBIT	$17.2	12.8	$220.2
EBDIT	$32.5	8.1	$263.3
DFE	$10.3	21.1	$217.3
DFCF	$25.6	9.6	$245.8
Median			$218.8
Selected			$215.0

Source: Werbalowsky and Stanford (1989).

certainty that now envelops Xcorp, allowing the company to solidify long-term relationships, which are necessary for future growth. Second, trade credit will be fully restored, improving working capital and cash flow. Third, management can focus on operations rather than on extraordinary financial-restructuring concerns. Finally, a morale boost from elimination of job-security concerns will improve efficiency.

Thus, it is not irrational to assume that Xcorp's value under the contemplated restructured capital structure is approximately $215 million.

Valuation of Xcorp's Individual Securities

Once Xcorp's enterprise value has been estimated, the individual securities must be valued. The first security class to be valued is equity, followed by senior secured debt. The subordinated debt and preferred stock are the final elements of the capital structure to be valued.

Equity Valuation

Several approaches may be used to value the equity in a distressed firm. First, the market approach may be used. Obviously, if the company is publicly held, the answer is determined by the market price, adjusted for controlling interest. This method may be complicated by decreased trading volume, investor confusion, general uncertainty in the publicly traded markets, and the fact that control premiums may increase dramatically in distressed situations in which control becomes the primary or sole value of equity. This technique is obviously more difficult for privately held companies whose common stock prices cannot be observed.

Second, assess the control value of equity. Equity is worth something, even in the most insolvent situations. Although difficult to quantify, a large component of aggregate equity value in distressed situations is attributable to control. Control allows a company to direct the workout process. The control value of equity can be estimated by determining the amount that senior creditors will pay the equityholders to "get out of their way." This is the present discounted value of their legal and other costs in divesting equity from its present position. In the example of Xcorp, we conclude that the maximum value for control ranges between $4.0 million and $6.0 million.

Third, the discounted cash flow approach can be used to value the equity position. This is very speculative to ascertain without deleveraging assumptions.

Fourth is the residual equity valuation. The residual approach subtracts the estimated market value of the securities in the capital structure from the company's enterprise value; the residual is the value of equity.

A fifth possibility is the option approach. Option pricing theory may be applied to equity valuation. Equity in an insolvent company may be analogized to an "out-of-the-money" call option on the assets of a company. The option value curve illustrated in **Figure 1** demonstrates how the value of the equity changes, given a change in the value of the company's assets.

The option pricing model requires five inputs: the value of the company's assets, the amount of outstanding senior claims, the volatility of asset values, the term (or length) of the option period, and the risk-free interest rate. The value of the assets is defined as the current market value of a company on an enterprise basis. This is analogous to the stock price. The exercise price is equal to the amount necessary to satisfy all senior claims (debt and preferred stock). To the extent that the earnings of the company are less than the interest and preferred dividends that accrue prior to exercise, this accrued amount is added to total senior claims and increases the exercise price (subject to bankruptcy law restrictions on such accrual). The volatility of the asset value is defined as the instantaneous variance of company asset values. This is difficult to measure directly; its value is generally derived from comparable companies. The term is the life of the option contract. Equity option value in a distressed situation exists until equity is divested of its rights to realize value from the company. The period ends when, for example, a senior lender forecloses on the company's assets, a creditor's plan of reorganization that eliminates equity is confirmed, or a company is liquidated. The risk-free rate is the yield to maturity for direct U.S. Treasury obligations with a term equal to the option's term.

Using this framework, **Table 10** shows that the approximate call value of Xcorp is $3.5 million.

In summary, equity value is calculated by comparing results obtained by at least three methods: the market-comparable, which generated a value of $6.8 million; the residual, which generated a value of $4.0 million; and the option pricing model, which generated a value of $3.5 million. Considering all of the above, Xcorp equity is valued at $5.0 million.

Senior Secured Debt Valuation

Valuation of the senior secured debt involves assessing the market prices of intercreditor trades,

---

Table 10. Modified Black-Scholes Option Pricing Model Assumptions for Equity Valuation, Pre-Exchange ($ in millions)

Fair market value of assets	$195.0
Book value of senior claims (debt plus preferred)	$334.0
Term (years)[1]	2.0
Volatility of asset returns[2]	25.0%
Risk-Free Rate	8.0%
Approximate call value	$ 3.5

Note: The modifications of the Black-Scholes Option Pricing Model result from applying the model to a range of assumptions distributed about the inputs illustrated above. This dynamic approach represents the treatment of variable strike price.

[1]Estimated time before which intransigent equity holders would be "wiped out" through secured lender foreclosure or confirmation of a creditors' Chapter 11 plan.

[2]This is probably an overestimation of volatility.

Source: Werbalowsky and Stanford (1989).

applying discounts to the face value of the notes, assessing the collateral coverage of the notes, analyzing the interest rates and terms, and assessing legal risk. Information on market prices of these instruments is difficult to get because they rarely trade, and to the extent they do, the information is generally not publicly available.

Several legal factors affect the $150.0 million face value of the notes. These include the following:

- *Lender liability risk*. In connection with this type of litigation threat, financial institutions may be receptive to modifications in the terms of their notes, which otherwise reduce their present value.
- *Equitable subordination risk*. If lenders have potential exposure to equitable subordination litigation and similar claims, value is reduced.
- *Fraudulent conveyance risk*. The much-discussed

Figure 1. The Relationship between the Equity Value and the Enterprise Value

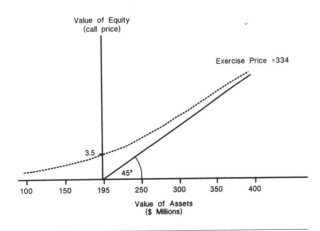

Source: Werbalowsky and Stanford (1989).

perils of lending transactions in which consideration ends up with someone other than the borrower (as often happens in LBOs) gives rise to the risk of, *inter alia*, avoidance of the creditor's security interest.

In the case of Xcorp, the lenders may be subject to a fraudulent conveyance attack; have reasonable interest rate, covenant protection, and collateral coverage; and are subject to a variety of payment-timing uncertainties. After some complex analysis, we determine that these factors suggest the appropriate market rate is 13 percent, resulting in a fair market value of $140 million, or a discount of 6.7 percent.

Valuation of Subordinated Debt and Preferred Stock

Valuation of the subordinated debt and preferred stock can only be equal to the residual value: the value remaining after subtracting the value of secured debt and equity from the company's enterprise value. If the firm is worth $195 million, equity is worth $5 million, and bank debt is worth $140 million, then the residual value is $50 million. Of course, a host of other techniques can be employed to directly value these securities as well. The allocation of the residual must be allocated among the preferred shareholders and subordinated debtholders using valuation approaches and qualitative factors deemed appropriate to represent some negotiated or imposed settlement. **Table 11** presents one approach, which targets recovery values based on the value allocation index (VAI).

The VAI measures the fairness of exchange—that is, the fair market value of the securities received in the exchange divided by the fair market value of the original securities. The VAI represents a more meaningful index of the exchange offer's fairness than an approach tied to the face amount of the securities.

Table 11 shows a value for the subordinated debt before the workout of $42, which is the status quo value of the subordinated debt, and of $50 after the workout, which is the value after restructuring.

Conclusion

Xcorp's difficulties occurred before the well-publicized financial crises of a host of textile-related companies, including WestPoint Pepperell, JPS Textile Group, Forstmann & Company, and Salant. The deterioration in the industry shows us, retrospectively, that even the most rigorous valuation techniques applied as recently as 1989 overstate what we now, in late 1990, believe are appropriate values. Thus, although the "snapshot" of a valuation process is often helpful, it is not a substitute for the continuous vision needed to appropriately evaluate distressed situations.

Although I have endeavored to determine security values with specificity in this example, recognize that substantial flexibility is necessary in interpreting these figures. Even in my relatively simple example, I could make strong arguments for materially different values. A full examination of all of the relevant issues certainly is necessary to assess value, but realization of value, based on numerous factors outside the realm of precise analysis, may yield materially different results. Sophisticated analysts realize that "staying on top" of the legal, economic, and interpersonal negotiating issues in distressed situations is necessary for continuing, accurate valuation.

Table 11. Fundamental Restructuring Analysis Based on a VAI Approach ($ in millions)

Components of Xcorp's Current Capital Structure[1]	Pre-Workout		Post-Workout	
	Face Value	Market Value	Target Market Value	Value Allocation Index
Senior secured	$150	$140	$140	1.00
Subordinated debt	107 [2]	42	50	1.19
Preferred stock	20 [3]	8	15	1.88
Common equity	10	5	10	2.00
	$287	$195	$215	

[1]Trade debt is not explicitly evaluated as a component of Xcorp's capital structure under this scenario. The size of this liability is considered in the valuation process through consideration of the level of working capital surplus/deficiency.

[2]Includes interest accrued through contemplated exchange date (July 1, 1989).

[3]Does not include underdeclared cumulative preferred dividends of $3.45 million.

Source: Werbalowsky and Stanford (1989).

Question and Answer Session

Question: Is the owner of 35 percent of the subordinated debt in Xcorp in an unassailable position to control the proceedings? Would a shift from Chapter 11 to Chapter 7 change the control?

Werbalowsky: In a Chapter 11 bankruptcy situation, two-thirds of the dollar amount of voting claims and more than one-half of the claims voting are required to have a class consent to a particular treatment. Therefore, if I have 35 percent of the bond debt, no one can make me accept an allocation I am not happy with, even if everyone else votes for it. That class might be subject to cram down, however, which is a complex way of confirming a plan despite the dissent of a class. The situation is different in a Chapter 7 proceeding. Chapter 7 is liquidation, and the trustee really does not care how much of the bond debt someone has. In a Chapter 7, no plan exists. The trustee will liquidate the assets and allocate them under the absolute priority rule, so once the company converts to Chapter 7, the interests of a subordinated debtholder with a controlling position in a class is not unassailable.

Question: Do you think the secured creditors of Resorts International gave up too much in the reorganization, especially in light of dimming business prospects?

Werbalowsky: No. A yes answer assumes that there is a unique value that can be obtained by senior or junior claimants. There was no unique settlement point in Resorts. The outcome depends on how good your negotiators are. They only give up too much if it is clearly a worse result than they could have obtained by litigating the entire matter on a present-value basis. I don't think that was the case in Resorts.

Question: How do you deal with the allocation among different tranches of subordinated debt?

Werbalowsky: This is the most difficult question in all of financial restructuring. Seniority gives you a better negotiating position in arguments, but it does not give you the full benefits of the subordination. It is nothing to negotiate banks against the debtor or the debtor against subordinated debt. It is much more difficult to get a deal when you are dealing with a couple of institutions that hold senior subordinated and junior subordinated. We have used a relative "step down" technique or our Value Allocation Index to reach settlement on our bondholder committees.

Case Histories: Success Versus Failure—The Advantage of Hindsight

David J. Breazzano
*President**
T. Rowe Price Recovery Fund Associates, Inc.

Investing in the securities of distressed and bankrupt companies is not for everyone. To be successful, you have to be opportunistic. I have been an opportunistic investor for most of my career.

Success in investing can be defined very simply: achieving an adequate return. It can also be defined as having a positive net present value when you discount at your hurdle rate what you ultimately receive upon the sale or liquidation of the investment. Failure is not achieving your hurdle rate on your investment.

The key to success is making the investment at the right price. The important issue is not whether it is a good or bad company; rather, it is the price at which you purchase the claim or security against the bankrupt company. For example, IBM is trading around $95 a share now; it would probably be a very good investment at $50 a share, and probably a poor investment at $200 a share. So we are not dealing with good or bad companies; we are dealing with good or bad *investments*, and that depends on whether the investment is available at an attractive price. In this presentation, I will discuss two cases and the keys to their success or the reasons for their failure.

Public Service Company of New Hampshire

The first case illustrates a successful investment in the bonds of Public Service Company of New Hampshire (PSCNH). **Figure 1** shows the trading pattern of PSCNH's 15-percent senior unsecured debentures due in the year 2003. These bonds are listed on the New York Exchange. Shortly after the Chapter 11 petition was filed in January of 1988, the debentures could have been purchased at below 30

cents on the dollar; today you could probably sell them close to 110 cents on the dollar, tripling your money in just a couple of years.

When a company starts getting into trouble, there often is a long period of publicized financial distress, which typically causes its securities to trade down. In the case of PSCNH, building the Seabrook Plant generated considerable adverse publicity. For a host of reasons there were delays, cost increases, and some other well-publicized maladies. When PSCNH could not get the plant on-line on a revised schedule, its securities began to trade down.

PSCNH was able to hold off financial disaster for a period of time, in part because the company was successful in raising money. It seemed to have an almost unlimited source of capital in public securities markets if it paid usurious rates of interest. Its last financing was a $100 million private placement that had close to a 20 percent interest rate. Eventually these financing sources ended.

Initially, the securities were held by more conservative investors—people who wanted to buy a bond and collect interest and principal in a timely fashion. All of a sudden the company defaulted and filed for protection under Chapter 11. The bondholders, such as high-yield mutual funds that needed to pay out a high dividend to attract shareholders, ended up with an equity-type security, which is not what most of them wanted to hold. They were unwilling holders who had to sell the bonds to the willing holders—the distressed investors, the vultures, and some other entities willing to hold non-interest bearing securities. That is a painful process. There are more sellers than buyers, and the buyers would not buy until the price was right—often a substantial discount.

This was a very big bankruptcy, so it required a lot of capital to absorb these bonds. As a result, they traded down too far; this created the investing opportunity. The initial low price of the securities reflected the fact that there was a gradual and painful transition from the unwilling holders to the willing

*Since the seminar, Mr. Breazzano moved to Fidelity Investments in Boston, where he is a Portfolio Manager emphasizing investments in high-yield and bankrupt securities and claims.

Figure 1. Trading Pattern of PSCNH's 15 Percent Senior Unsecured Debentures (Due in 2003)

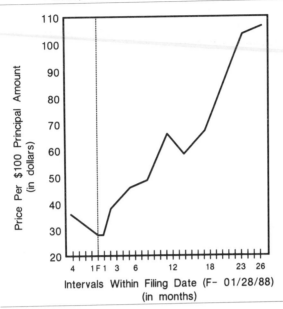

holders. Ultimately, as people realized the values were significantly greater than zero, the bonds traded up.

One of the things that led to a lower price than was justified by fundamental values was the high level of uncertainty surrounding the first utility bankruptcy since the 1930s. There were a lot of uncertainties regarding the legal issues, such as rate regulation versus the bankruptcy code, and so forth. It was complex. People did not want to take the time to try to understand it—and it may not even have been possible to understand because there was no recent precedent.

Three factors contributed to the bankruptcy. The inability to bring Seabrook on-line within a reasonable time frame was one factor. Seabrook was something like 10 to 15 years behind schedule and 10 times over budget. Under New Hampshire law there is an anti-CWIP (construction work in progress) provision, so PSCNH could not recover any costs until Seabrook was up and running. So here was this small New Hampshire utility that had over 60 percent of its assets non-income producing and financed at an exorbitant cost of capital. PSCNH could not collect any return on 60 percent of its assets, so eventually the ball game was over.

I think the Chernobyl nuclear plant disaster, which occurred in April of 1986, was another factor that contributed to the bankruptcy of Public Service Company of New Hampshire. Before that accident, the general consensus was that the company would be able to get Seabrook on-line before it exhausted its

ability to tap the public securities markets, perhaps 1987 or 1988 at the latest. The company was able to borrow to fund itself prior to 1986. The Chernobyl accident changed the sentiment about nuclear plants in general and, more specifically, created a lot of uncertainty about when PSCNH could bring Seabrook on-line—if, in fact, it ever could.

The third factor that contributed to the bankruptcy was the presidential campaign of 1988. The governor of Massachusetts, Michael Dukakis, had to have a good showing in the New Hampshire primary. The democrats in New Hampshire were mostly anti-nuclear. Dukakis, probably for political reasons, embarked on a campaign to frustrate the ultimate licensing of the plant, stating that he was concerned that the Massachusetts communities near the New Hampshire border could not be evacuated in the event of a nuclear emergency. About 10 towns, in theory, would have had to be evacuated if there was such an emergency. This is a curious reaction considering that the Pilgrim Nuclear Plant had been operating at the base of Cape Cod for years; wouldn't it be more difficult to evacuate Cape Cod than to evacuate 10 towns on the fringe of Massachusetts?

Analysis of Public Service Company of New Hampshire

The company was pushed into Chapter 11 for what I think were purely financial reasons. PSCNH is a legal monopoly. It is allowed by law to receive an adequate return on its investment. There were no major operational problems, so there was no need to bring in a turnaround specialist to make electricity better. Quite simply, the problem was that debt-service requirements were too high. Because of the previously mentioned complexities, the market overreacted to the bankruptcy.

We were not as pessimistic as most investors. We felt that Seabrook would ultimately come on-line. The main factor in Seabrook's favor was that New England was a capacity-constrained area that needed the electricity. There were no other plants under construction that could handle the load requirements that the area was going to grow into.

Under New Hampshire law, PSCNH was allowed to put the entire Seabrook investment into its rate base when Seabrook came on-line. Practically speaking, however, it could not increase rates by 30 to 40 percent in one year without people looking for alternative energy sources. But PSCNH would be in the driver's seat as far as negotiating a rate increase with the Public Service Commission in New Hampshire. Another consideration was whether PSCNH could get away from New Hampshire rate regulations. Under Federal regulations, perhaps there would be some allowance for better rate relief, which would enhance values. We felt that PSCNH had that type of flexibility, or at least the threat of that flexibility, under the bankruptcy code. The threat alone, in our opinion, gave it leverage with rate makers and other constituencies.

In addition, we felt that nuclear energy is fairly safe. On a statistical basis, there have been more deaths in coal mining accidents than in nuclear accidents in this country. Other countries (such as France) use nuclear power extensively and successfully. Furthermore, Seabrook has state-of-the-art technology. Its design is totally different from Chernobyl.

It is important to analyze the downside—the scenario without Seabrook. In our opinion, PSCNH was basically sound. It had a strong, stable cash flow. Based on historical data and projections, the entity could throw off $120 to $130 million annually in cash flow, excluding all Seabrook-related expenses and projected revenue. That is somewhat unrealistic, however, because PSCNH was going to continue to fund the construction and maintenance of Seabrook, so its real free cash flow would not be that high over the next several years. The company's first, second, and third mortgage bonds had required interest payments of approximately $80 million, so without Seabrook it had cash flow available for the senior unsecured debentures.

Valuation of the Bonds
We tried to determine how much the bonds might be worth. We looked at cash-flow forecasts from different scenarios. The average coupon in this company was 14 to 15 percent. So we looked at the scenario where the average coupon was cut in half. What if PSCNH had 8 percent bonds outstanding and it was a BBB-rated company? In that case, the bonds would probably trade close to par. Alternatively, what if the unsecured debt had a 5 percent coupon? In the end, we were comfortable that in a worst-case scenario we would get at least 50 cents on the dollar for these bonds. They were trading at 28 cents on the dollar at the time, so we had a lot of downside protection.

It was not sufficient, however, only to look at PSCNH's current cash flow. There were other things it could do, such as sell assets. For example, what if it sold a coal fire plant to a Maine utility? PSCNH has a number of older facilities that are on its books for significantly less than replacement cost. These assets are in the rate base at cost, not replacement value. If the company sold one of these assets to another entity outside of that state's jurisdiction, the asset would go into that entity's rate base at that

entity's cost, which would provide a significant profit to PSCNH. In addition, if PSCNH could get some rate relief, the financial position would be stronger. These possibilities could enhance values significantly above 50 cents on the dollar to senior unsecured securities.

The Bankruptcy
PSCNH filed for bankruptcy protection on January 28, 1988. The filing was triggered by an indentured trustee's attempt to attach assets in response to the company's failure to make interest payments on certain public issues. The company had tried to reorganize out of court, but its situation was such a complicated matter and required certain rate relief that the State of New Hampshire was reluctant to give. Therefore, PSCNH had no alternative but to file under Chapter 11.

The bankruptcy was characterized by certain legal maneuvering. For example, during the proceedings PSCNH asked for a declaratory judgment as to what rates it could be allowed to charge. That remains an open issue, because a consensual plan developed before the hearing could be held.

Adequate-protection issues were addressed in the case. PSCNH had first mortgage bonds, general and refunding bonds (second mortgages), and third mortgage bonds. Simply put, adequate protection is where a secured creditor seeks to foreclose on its collateral, or, if that is denied, to either be paid interest or to have the interest accrue. In this case, the judge allowed PSCNH to continue paying interest during the bankruptcy on the first and second mortgages.

The first and second mortgage bonds were great conservative investments. How much risk was there? The worst had happened; the company was bankrupt. Yet, the markets still felt there was some additional risk. As a result, the bonds could be purchased at a discount for some time following the petition, although the holders continued to receive timely interest payments throughout the proceeding.

The third mortgages ultimately recovered the full claim amount. These bonds did not receive interest on a current basis, but at the end of the case they received 100 cents on the dollar plus postpetition interest; so, in a sense, they were adequately protected. The judge did not want current interest payments made on the third mortgages because he felt there was a margin for error. In his opinion, the bondholders had nothing to worry about because there was an adequate cushion and they would get interest at the end of the proceeding, even though interest was being paid on the first and second mortgages in the interim.

The Outcome

During the proceeding it became apparent that PSCNH might be acquired by a third party. Therefore, the court needed some guidance as to the estate's value. A court-appointed examiner estimated that PSCNH's assets were worth at least $2.2 billion. There was about $1.7 billion of total debt, which meant the debt was covered 100 percent and the preferred stock and common stock were entitled to the balance.

A bidding war developed for the company involving over a dozen entities—some serious, some not—who were interested in buying the assets. Ultimately, Northeast Utilities prevailed with the highest bid of approximately $2.3 billion. This transaction is still pending, but ultimately the 15 percent debentures due 2003 are entitled to receive a combination of cash and stock. The stock will be retired for cash when Northeast Utilities completes the merger, resulting in proceeds to the debentures in excess of 110 cents on the dollar.

There are several reasons PSCNH was attractive to these other utilities. First, the replacement costs of the company's assets were significantly higher than the cost at which the entire company could be acquired through a bankruptcy auction. Another utility could acquire PSCNH at prices that would allow it to generate electricity below the acquiring utility's average cost, so it made economic sense for other utilities in the region to pay more for those assets than the book value of PSCNH. Second, Seabrook was coming on-line, despite some false starts.

About this time, the State of New Hampshire realized that it would be at a disadvantage in negotiating rates after Seabrook came on-line because of the significant increase in PSCNH's rate base. The state decided to negotiate a limit on rate increases for New Hampshire residents in advance of Seabrook commencing operations. To win the state's endorsement of its acquisition of PSCNH, Northeast Utilities agreed to the limit of a 5.5 percent annual rate increase for the next seven years, plus other arrangements for fuel cost adjustments, and so forth.

There are risks involved with any successful investment. For PSCNH, the risk was that Seabrook would not come on-line, combined with not being able to raise rates. Risks are always present, but in hindsight, the risks were not that great in this case.

Liquor Barn

The Liquor Barn leveraged buyout (LBO) illustrates an investment failure. The company's $25 million private placement was wiped out following its Chapter 11 filing.

Liquor Barn, originally a division of Safeway Stores, operated a chain of over 100 discount liquor stores, primarily in California. In 1987, Safeway divested Liquor Barn. Majestic Wines, a British firm, paid more than $100 million for the division, outbidding the unit's management. This ultimately spelled disaster. Majestic Wines was a holding company that owned 100 percent of the common stock of the Liquor Barn operating entities. The deal was financed with about $70 million of bank debt, which was issued at the holding company level, but received secured guarantees by the operating entity. The private placement notes, also issued by the holding company, did not receive a similar guarantee. Equity of about $15 million was provided by Majestic.

Majestic Wines thought it knew how to run the liquor business better than the former management of Liquor Barn. Majestic also felt it could justify paying $100 million for the company because it could generate more cash flow out of the operations. Consequently, Majestic proceeded to change the marketing strategy for the company to make it a more upscale liquor retailer; their main marketing gambit was to have wine and cheese parties at their stores. The problem was that Liquor Barn was a discount retailer with a lower margin business. The high-end people did not shop there, and they did not want to shop there just because there was a wine and cheese party. The traditional customers did not like the new upscale French wines that were being sold; they bought California wines. So the franchise was ruined: Instead of going up, the cash flow went down; the values deteriorated; trade creditors ultimately put it on a COD basis; the banks threatened to call its loans; and the company ended up going into bankruptcy.

In the liquor business, companies make most of their money around Christmas and New Year's Day, so they need adequate inventory on their shelves or they are going to miss the season. Liquor Barn's trade creditors were requiring cash on delivery, but it had no cash. Liquor Barn was forced to file for bankruptcy protection on November 15, 1988, to get a debtor-in-possession loan so that it could restock its shelves and try to continue business.

It was tough turning this company around because new management had destroyed its business franchise and its cash flow had deteriorated. The trade creditors and the banks who had a guarantee from the operating entities were not interested in trying to turn the company around. They were not interested in taking an equity position—they wanted cash. A financial advisor was retained to find bidders for the assets. It was felt it would be better to sell the entire business to another entity that could run it better than the current management and to cash-out the lenders.

Majestic Wines ended up selling the business for about $40 million, including inventory. A company that once had 104 stores and 1,000 employees ended up with about 75 stores and 800 employees. The company was sold en masse as a going concern with a few exceptions. It was sold en masse for two reasons. First, the trade creditors were interested in keeping it a going concern as opposed to a piecemeal liquidation because Liquor Barn was their largest customer. Therefore, they were willing to take less value on their claim if they could sell it as a going concern and continue to do business with the company. Second, the banks were not particularly interested in trying to reorganize the company; they wanted cash, not equity.

The holding company was in a very difficult situation because although the Liquor Barn retailing entities filed under Chapter 11, the holding company never did. In fact, I learned of this case through a bankruptcy attorney friend who represented the holding company private placement noteholders. He said, "I have a really strange case: a bankrupt company that is not a debtor. My entity is not in bankruptcy. It is not paying any interest, but it did not file. The operating entity is in Chapter 11. A creditors' committee has been appointed, the banks are doing their thing, they have their lawyers, and are all up to speed. And here we are outside Chapter 11 with fewer rights and no standing in the case."

Later, the attorney had to file an involuntary Chapter 11 petition to put the holding company into bankruptcy. The holding company, however, only owned the equity of the operating company, and therefore was structurally subordinated to the banks and the trade creditors. The lawyer tried a legal mechanism to elevate the status of the holding company noteholders, trying to claim that the two entities were really one company. He claimed that because it was operated as one, the $25 million private placement notes were as much a claim at the operating level as the trade and bank debt.

The judge denied that argument, however. A reorganization plan subsequently was confirmed, dividing the operating entity's assets between the banks and the trade creditors, but providing no recovery to the holding company. Consequently, in this case, the holding company creditors recovered nothing.

To add insult to injury, the estate is now suing the private placement holders to recover an interest payment made within 90 days before the Chapter 11 petition. So not only did these creditors recover zero, they may get less than zero as a result of the Chapter 11 petition if the bankruptcy court forces them to return this interest payment.

Conclusion

In this business you have to do a lot of homework, understand corporate structure and business problems, and have patience. If the appropriate price is not available (and sometimes that price is zero), be prepared to walk away.

Question and Answer Session

Question: Is the Liquor Barn holding company lawyer still your friend?

Breazzano: Surprisingly so. What I failed to mention is that when he alerted me to this situation I ended up buying a lot of the trade claims and became the largest trade creditor in that case, so he is particularly annoyed that I made a big profit on the reorganization, while he got wiped out. But you find investment opportunities any way you can.

Question: In the Liquor Barn case, did the guarantee's collateral prove valuable to the banks?

Breazzano: Not really, because there was an issue of fraudulent conveyance. The operating entity, Liquor Barn retailing subsidiaries, did not receive any value by virtue of the banks lending the $70 million. The $70 million went directly to the old shareholder of Liquor Barn, which was Safeway Stores. Therefore the entity that the trade creditors had claims against received no value. The banks' guarantee was secured, which technically should have given them priority over the trade creditors absent the fraudulent conveyance issue.

There were some other issues. In California you cannot pledge alcoholic beverages as collateral. Consequently, about $15 to $20 million of inventory value could not have been pledged to the banks and, therefore, would have been available to the trade and the banks equally. But the leasehold interest and so forth, which were valuable, could have been given over to the banks.

The trade creditors were also motivated by preserving the entity. They wanted to continue to sell products to Liquor Barn, and they were afraid that if they pursued the litigation, which would have been funded by the estate, and ultimately prevailed and subordinated the banks, maybe they would get 100 cents on their claims, but Liquor Barn would have gone out of business. It did not have the cash flow to fund that type of litigation, and the business would have disintegrated because it would not have been able to stock its shelves for the following Christmas and New Year's season. So it was ul-

timately compromised such that the banks and the trade creditors were essentially treated equal.

Question: It has been said that par bondholders should welcome vulture funds and new buyers because they will, in some ways, contribute to recovery on the part of par bondholders. Is that your view?

Breazzano: Yes. I agree with that wholeheartedly. Several factors contribute to this situation. The biggest factor is what I call lender fatigue. The par buyers, the people who have been in a situation for several years before it became troubled, get very fatigued and frustrated by the whole case. As the company continues in bankruptcy, the par buyers are willing to accept a lot less than what they are entitled to if it comes in the form of cash and allows them just to go away. In contrast, the so-called vultures that come in after the fact are a little fresher. They are willing to wait for a fair deal.

My firm invests in bankruptcies to make money. We think we know how to restructure companies and find solutions to complex issues and bring fresh insight to the table, and maybe some new ideas. Even if we buy a claim at 20 to 30 cents on the dollar, we are going to fight to get 100 cents or more—whatever we are entitled to. The profits that you make on the good investments offset some of the Liquor Barns of the world.

My experience is that the par creditors are much more inclined to take less at the end of the day. I have been through 30 or 40 Chapter 11 proceedings, and invariably at the end of the day it is the par creditors, people who have been in it longer, who are much more willing to compromise and accept a little bit less than what they could recover, just to get out.

Question: What are your favorite bonds right now?

Breazzano: I think the Resorts International Showboat Lease Passthrough bonds will be a good investment. The company is coming out of Chapter 11 now. It was a fairly clean Chapter 11. Based on my reading of the disclosure statement and on the price at which you could purchase the bonds today, I believe you could achieve fairly attractive future returns.

The Institutional Investor Perspective

Dean J. Takahashi

Director of Endowment Management
Yale University

In this presentation, I will use the Yale Endowment Fund as an illustration of the approach an institutional investor might take in considering investing in distressed securities. I will discuss how Yale developed the investment program for its endowment and describe how the university evaluates and selects managers and analyzes the structure of investment vehicles. It should be noted that the analysis and planning process used to develop an investment program in distressed securities can also be applied to other areas of investment. In fact, our work in distressed securities reflects the general approach we take toward any new investment opportunity.

Yale University Endowment

Yale University Endowment, a $2.5 billion fund, was established in the 1700s to support the school's educational mission and academic program. The fund pays out approximately 4.5 percent of its market value annually to help cover operating costs. Returns above the spending rate are reinvested to help preserve the purchasing value of the endowment principal.

The need to achieve a real return of at least 4.5 percent leads Yale to a predominantly equity-oriented investment policy. This is reflected in the endowment's asset allocation. Approximately 80 percent of the fund is allocated to equities of one form or another; only 20 percent is allocated to fixed-income investments. We do not attempt to time markets; instead, we try to control risk by emphasizing diversification across different types of equities. Our policy targets are established across five asset classes: 45 percent in domestic equities, 15 percent in foreign equities, 10 percent in private equities (for example, venture capital and leveraged buyouts), 10 percent in equity real estate, and 20 percent in fixed income (principally U.S. government bonds).

Yale is unusual in that it has only 65 percent of its target asset allocation in U.S. stocks, bonds, and cash, and 35 percent in what might be termed alternative investments. In comparison, most institutional portfolios tend to have more than 90 percent of their assets in U.S. stocks, bonds, and cash, and less than 10 percent in alternative asset classes.

In recognition of the university's need to achieve high real returns and increase the diversification of its investments, we have frequently exploited emerging opportunities before they became widely accepted by the institutional investment community. For instance, Yale began investing in leveraged buyouts in 1973, venture capital in 1976, equity real estate in 1978, and foreign equities in 1980. A willingness to move early into unconventional investments has helped the endowment's performance. Leveraged buyouts and venture capital investments have generated a rate of return of more than 30 percent since inception. Our real estate and foreign equity investments have produced returns in excess of 20 percent per year. Overall, Yale's annualized performance has topped 17 percent over the past five- and ten-year periods, placing the fund's performance in the top decile of large institutional funds.

Yale's exposure to distressed securities investments began in the mid-1980s when one of our active managers began taking opportunistic positions in bankruptcies such as Manville and Storage Technology. In early 1988, we began developing an investment program to diversify our domestic equity exposure by increasing use of nontraditional investment strategies such as short selling, merger arbitrage, and distressed securities. Our interest in distressed securities was partly a response to what we saw as the overleveraging of corporate America, the increased rate of bankruptcies, the likelihood of a softening of the economy, and the evidence of high return potential in distressed securities.

Currently, we have three managers with specific mandates to invest significant portions of their portfolios in distressed situations, and two other managers who invest in them when opportunities arise. At present we have approximately $30 million invested in distressed situations; we are willing to invest up to $75 million, or roughly 3 percent of the endowment.

Nature of Investment Opportunity

Before investing in distressed securities, it is important to define them—to describe their investment characteristics and determine why you are interested in investing in them. The definition should be broad; it should include not only companies in bankruptcy, but also those that are heading into bankruptcy (or are thought to be), those emerging from reorganization, and those in any other financially distressed situation. Generally speaking, the investment objectives, analysis, and skills involved are the same for all. Restricting oneself to a narrow definition of bankruptcy limits the investment opportunities and the timing of getting in and out of certain bankruptcy plays. It is also important to be flexible in choosing which investment instruments are appropriate—for example, equities, equity derivatives, debt securities, bank notes, or other private claims. It also helps to be able to go either long or short and to use related instruments to hedge investments.

The investment opportunities in distressed situations vary over time. In the early and mid-1980s, the universe of financially distressed companies was relatively small. Today, using a broad definition of distressed securities, the market is large, and it could grow larger if the economy weakens further. Edward Altman's (1990) research indicates that the market value of distressed securities might be as high as $200 billion and growing.

Theoretically, investing in the heavily discounted debt of a bankrupt company could be considered similar to a leveraged, covered call position. The position is highly volatile and sensitive to the overall value of the firm, just like a leveraged stock position. In addition, one's return might be capped at the par value of the bond plus its accrued interest. That value is analogous to the strike price of the call you have written. If such securities were fairly and efficiently valued, it would be hard to justify their role in an institutional portfolio. Therefore, you should not invest in distressed securities unless you believe there is an exploitable market inefficiency.

There are two potential sources of excess risk-adjusted returns to distressed securities: First, the entire market for distressed securities might be broadly undervalued, and second, the market may provide opportunities for one to consistently outperform and add value through active management.

There are several reasons to suspect that the market for distressed securities is undervalued. Filing for bankruptcy—even the expectation of a Chapter 11 filing—frightens away many investors who base their investment decisions on the predictability of future earnings of the company. The analysis of bankruptcies is quite complex. Many lenders and portfolio managers prefer to sell debt at a huge discount than to face uncertain resumption of payment and the potential embarrassment of holding bankrupt securities. Some institutional investors are required by investment guidelines or capital requirements to sell holdings of distressed companies. These factors can create strong selling pressure incommensurate with the underlying security values.

Although there may be evidence that the distressed securities market has generated superior returns in the past, those returns could easily evaporate or reverse in the future. The investors who previously sold automatically at the first sign of distress may choose to hold onto their securities in the future when the stigma is gone and they see the high returns generated by those who bought from them. Then, prices will have less upward potential upon reorganization because they did not drop as low as in the past.

Alternatively, if the economy deteriorates significantly, the liquidated or reorganized value of distressed companies could drop at the same time the number of bankruptcies swamp the court system, thereby extending the time to reorganization. Delays cause returns to decline because of the time value of money and the deterioration of the underlying business operating in bankruptcy.

In a healthy market scenario (one with less financial distress), many investors may invest in distress, driving up prices as they become committed to the market when opportunities are limited. Over the short term, a depressed economy or a dropping stock market might produce a dramatic increase in the supply of distressed securities. Prices might drop across the board as sellers vastly outnumber potential buyers at current values. Selling pressure might be generated by changes in governmental regulations concerning insurance companies or pension plans. Although some of these scenarios will generate long-term buying opportunities, returns will probably suffer in the short term until deals have successfully reorganized.

The other possibility for excess returns is generated by superior portfolio management. The analysis of distressed companies is extremely complex and requires a broader set of skills than ordinary equity or fixed-income research. For example, one must have a detailed knowledge of the assets and liabilities on and off the balance sheet; one must calculate the value of the firm as a going concern and on a liquidated basis; and one must understand the legal mechanisms of bankruptcy and the potential latitude of court decisions. In addition, knowing the objectives and inclinations of leading players in a bankruptcy can help an investor understand behind-the-scenes negotiations that are often critical to the ultimate plan of reorganization.

Because of the difficulties and costs of producing a thorough analysis of financially distressed companies, and because there is not a high demand among investors for such research, most Wall Street analysts do not cover firms after they become distressed. Furthermore, the potential for rapid change in operations, negotiations, and court rulings can quickly render old information obsolete. Therefore, investors with good information sources and analytical skills have advantages over those who are less knowledgeable.

Investment opportunities in distressed situations span a wide variety of securities, each of which will be affected differently and not necessarily in obvious ways by the company's reorganization or liquidation. Developing an understanding of the differences among the securities of a distressed company is another labor-intensive task. Again, the investor with skill and vigor has the competitive advantage.

The importance of analytical skills and understanding is magnified by the diversity of security holders in distressed situations. They may include vendors with trade claims, bank lenders, bondholders, stockholders, and specialized bankruptcy fund managers. The investment objectives, risk tolerances, information, and expertise of each security holder vary tremendously. The ability to add value is made easier by the presence of others who are prone to giving up value.

Investment Characteristics

The range of investments makes it very difficult to generalize distressed securities as a single homogeneous asset class. An investment can be very low risk, for example a well-collateralized secured note that generates a high yield, or it can be very high risk, for example an equity holding where it is possible to lose virtually all of one's investment. In most cases, however, distressed investments should be considered equity investments regardless of the underlying security.

It would be a mistake to consider an investment in distressed bonds as part of a fixed-income portfolio. The value and payoff of a discounted debt security of a company in bankruptcy is not fixed, but rather is a function of the value of the firm. In one sense, pure fixed-income securities have no credit risk and no call risk. Although investment-grade bonds have some equity risk, their returns are primarily a function of interest rate fluctuations. In contrast, the returns of distressed securities are most strongly linked to the bankruptcy proceedings and the economic prospects of the issuing corporation.

In many instances, returns to investments in defaulted bonds tend to be more dependent on deal-specific issues and the assets of the company rather than a market multiple and the company's future earnings. Consequently, returns are not tightly linked to stock market returns. Research by Altman (1990) and actual returns of managers confirm this lack of correlation with the stock market. This diversification is certainly attractive to the institutional investor, but one should not expect immunity from any major downturn in the stock market (which reflects a significant revaluation of corporate assets).

Most investments in distressed securities are illiquid. When a company enters into distress and the price, market value, and trading volume of its publicly traded securities fall, transaction costs and illiquidity rise. Furthermore, many of the most attractive positions in a bankruptcy are private claims that are even more difficult to find, negotiate, and trade.

Distressed investments can be made with a variety of expectations regarding corporate governance. One approach is to acquire a controlling position in a workout situation. Another approach is to take an active involvement in negotiating the plans for reorganization. At the other extreme, one can trade distressed securities without exerting influence or control over the corporate decisions.

Distressed securities differ from most public stock and bond investments because they afford investors the opportunity to control risk and add value through active involvement. Identifying and negotiating the purchase of private claims such as bank debt and trade claims can generate investments superior to those available in the public markets. Once an investment is made, active negotiations, litigation, and coordinated action can significantly boost and accelerate the realization of returns. Through active negotiations, investors can ensure that securities received as a result of restructuring are unrestricted and freely tradeable, providing a quick and simple route to liquidity.

In summary, there appear to be opportunities to generate high risk-adjusted returns by investing in the securities of financially distressed companies. One should keep in mind, however, that the returns are subject to macro-level supply and demand conditions that may lead to limited opportunities and potentially poor investment results over significant periods of time. Fortunately, much of the risk in distressed investments is specific to each deal. Experience and superior assessment of risk and return trade-offs should be helpful in avoiding disasters and limiting downside exposure.

Suitability for the Yale Endowment

The Yale Endowment has several characteristics that make it well suited to participate in distressed securities. First, no current or prospective regulatory requirements prohibit the endowment from investing in bankrupt situations. Second, the endowment's large size and low payout requirements allow it to maintain significant portfolios of liquid assets. Third, the university's long investment horizon allows it to take positions in investments that may underperform over short periods of time. Fourth, Yale's Investments Office is large enough to afford the time and energy to conduct a comprehensive review of managers and monitor performance on an ongoing basis. Fifth, the university's governing board and administration is comfortable taking positions in unconventional investments. Sixth, the endowment is small enough to make appropriately sized yet meaningful commitments of capital to managers.

Attempting to match the opportunity with the university's strengths as an institutional investor, we designed our investment program in distressed securities with the following characteristics:

- Invest only with superior management to best exploit inefficiencies, control risk, and add value. Focus on managers who have a good global sense of risk and opportunity and who are interested in developing a long-term working relationship.
- Give managers a broad mandate, and facilitate their judgments to reduce or increase their participation in the distressed market relative to other opportunities. Provide the flexibility of funding levels to meet fluctuating investment conditions and enable managers to alter exposure to markets that are obviously over- or under-valued.
- Control against poor manager selection by diversifying across several managers, and try to avoid investments that effectively lock-up assets and prohibit changing managers.
- Use the managers to deepen our understanding of the distressed market and its participants.

One can see that the Yale investment approach to distressed securities is not appropriate for many institutional investors. In relation to the assets employed, we spend a disproportionate amount of time in this arena—meeting, reviewing, and working with managers. This would not be feasible for a fund with a small investment staff. We choose to dedicate time to opportunities such as distressed securities because these areas of inefficiency allow us the greatest opportunity to add value by choosing superior management strategies. Of course, asset allocation and a broad policy are most important, but exploiting market inefficiencies can make the difference between good and superior fund performance.

Manager Selection

The first question to resolve in choosing a manager is whether to hire an external manager or manage the funds internally. At Yale, our first inclination is to use outside managers. We do not have the skills or experience within our office to invest with a competitive advantage. Developing the talent in-house would be costly, and there would be considerable risk that if the manager were any good, he or she might leave for a more lucrative position. Further, if performance or market conditions were poor, it would be more difficult to take investment responsibilities away from an internal manager rather than an external one.

When we consider external managers, we look at several key factors. First and foremost, we are concerned with the quality of the people—obviously a very subjective assessment. We look for integrity, credibility, intelligence, experience, and judgment. In general, we are looking for people we can trust; people with a long-term investor mentality, who are not fee oriented or transaction driven. We like to see our managers invest their own money alongside ours. We derive our judgments from multiple discussions and meetings with managers and visits to their offices. When there is a team of people, we look for complementary skills and personalities, and for good interpersonal dynamics between the principals.

We verify our assessments by checking the references provided by the managers; we also talk to others we feel have some insight into their ability and character. We try to solicit views from people who have dealt with the managers from a variety of perspectives—former partners, investment clients, lawyers, company managements, and other principals in the investment community. We pay close attention to the quality of people who affiliate themselves with a manager. In checking references, it is particularly important to listen to what is not said, as well as to what is explicitly expressed. All of these precautions are vital because institutions must be concerned with the ethics and legalities of a manager's investment operation, especially in the distressed arena. Not only does the institution risk being victimized by shady dealings, but mere association with bad characters can be extremely embarrassing and damaging.

After the quality of the people, the next most important consideration is the investment strategy of the manager. We look for approaches that make sense long term and that take advantage of the manager's skills and resources to exploit opportunities. If the manager is attempting to take operating control of a company, we want to see good negotiating skills, operating expertise, and experience in the management team. If the manager is employing a diversified-portfolio approach, we like to see strong analytical skills, good information sources, and the ability to assess and control portfolio risk.

A manager's strategy should also be consistent with the amount of assets under management. For instance, a concentrated blocking position in a defaulted bond requires considerable capital and bears tremendous idiosyncratic risk and very little liquidity. The manager should have a large capital base and significant diversification through other investments to attempt this strategy. Otherwise, a snag in the deal could cause him tremendous pain and stress. A diversified portfolio manager should have enough assets to cover the expense of having enough analysts to analyze and trade, but eventually, size can be restrictive in establishing and liquidating meaningful positions in the portfolio.

Another important consideration in judging a management's team is its track record. In reviewing a performance record, it is particularly important to consider it in relation to your assessment of the people and their investment strategy. Do the investment results demonstrate that the team did execute the proposed strategy? Summary numbers of high returns are encouraging, but they are not a sufficient basis for investment decision, particularly in areas as dynamic as distressed securities investing. Of course, performance should always be considered in relation to the amount of assets under management and the team that was in place when they were generated.

Evaluating investment performance records in distressed situations is complicated by a number of factors. Before the recent rash of financial distress, bankruptcies were relatively rare and isolated events. Typically, those who invested in distressed companies were, by necessity, opportunistic, and thus lacked identifiable track records in this area. Return information tends to be anecdotal, deal specific, and very hard—if not impossible—to verify. The difficulties in evaluating past investments is compounded by the diversity of approaches and investment strategies. Without assessing the level of risk a manager assumes to achieve his track record, evaluation and performance on a risk-adjusted basis is problematic. Finally, the lack of any benchmark return or any manager universe data makes it hard to compare returns on a quantitative basis.

There are two other issues that can present serious obstacles when considering managers: problems in organizational stability and conflicts of interest. Because the most important consideration is people, we are very concerned that the people we choose as investment principals will be in place for a long time. We are wary of large organizations that view people as interchangeable and routinely shift personnel around to meet the needs of the firm. We are also concerned when profits generated by the investment principals are channeled to other areas. If the principals feel they are not justly rewarded, they may leave the company and thereby negate our reasons for selecting the firm. Therefore, it is important to ask about past turnover of people in the firm.

Conflicts of interest present additional concern. The primary focus and mission of the firm should be managing portfolio investments. Investors should look carefully at related activities, with particular attention given to brokerage and other fee-generating businesses. For instance, a lucrative brokerage operation may inhibit a manager from taking an active value-added approach that will lead to trading restrictions.

Structure of Investment Vehicles

When it comes to the structure of investment vehicles, we have no hard and fast rules, except that we try to keep the manager's and our interests aligned. With greater coincidence of interest, the manager has less incentive to act in ways that may be harmful to the investor. This is one important reason we like to see our managers invest a large portion of their own money alongside our endowment's. The mutual investment leads the manager to invest as a principal with due consideration toward risk. In addition, the manager's focus on return rather than management fees tends to dampen interest in expanding assets under management to a point where returns might suffer. For similar reasons we like to see our investment managers directly rewarded for their work, preferably as owners of their investment business. This position of ownership promotes stability and interest in preserving long-term relationships with us.

Because of fluctuating market conditions, we have been especially interested in separate accounts; they allow our managers to invest in areas other than distressed securities when opportunities are limited, and they allow us to increase funding when rewarding investments are abundant. In terms of the level of fees, again, we have no hard and fast rule except that the compensation should be fair and in keeping with industry standards. We try to avoid people who claim to be so exceptional that they are worthy of a special fee. All too many times that indicates greediness and too much focus on managing for fees rather than a return on investments.

Because we put so much effort into trying to choose first-rate managers, we expect to receive good value by paying industry norms. In the area of distress, however, it is difficult to identify that norm. Managers in distressed securities have come from a variety of investment backgrounds, often with entirely different fee structures. Some charge a percentage of assets under management and others take a carried interest of profits. Obviously, all other things being equal, it is preferable to pay the lower fee. However, it is more important to get the best management and for them to be fairly compensated. After all, it is the net after-fee, risk-adjusted return that really matters. That is the number that we hope will be highest for Yale.

Question and Answer Session

Question: Where do you get the names of potential managers?

Takahashi: We talk to people. We talk to people who are involved in distressed situations and ask them who they respect and who they work with, and then we go and meet those people. If you wait around in your office, you will not find a lot of the people who are doing the best work.

Question: How does investment in distressed securities differ from a contrarian investment strategy across the board?

Takahashi: The primary difference is that most contrarian strategies are in relatively efficient markets such as the stock market, and our approach in distressed investments is to exploit inefficiencies to get excess returns.

Question: To the extent that investors in distressed securities eventually have some influence on the outcome of the workout, does this represent a reduction in the variability of returns, and in that sense a reduction of risk? If that is true, should we not expect a gradual reduction in the rate of return on these securities to reflect that reduction in uncertainty?

Takahashi: In some instances, skilled investors may be able to expedite negotiations and accelerate reaching agreement on a plan for reorganization. Early resolution can improve returns for most, if not all, investors. One might expect the consequent excess risk-adjusted returns to attract more capital into distressed situations. On the other hand, the influence some investors exert on the investment outcome of a bankruptcy often comes at the expense of other investors. In these instances, the total risk is not reduced; it is borne by the less skilled investors. Thus, investment risk may actually increase for the marginal investor.

Question: What do you look for in a manager's track record?

Takahashi: The track record must be considered generally and with some skepticism. It is very difficult to find an isolated set of returns that reflects a focused approach in distress. It is more important to have an understanding of the management team and their strategy, and to see that the track record shows instances where the managers executed their strategy, controlled risk, and perhaps added value to their investments. Nonetheless, distressed securities represent a very dynamic market, and even if the past returns were quite good it is not necessarily an indication that future returns will be as good.

Reference List

Altman, E. 1968. "Financial Ratios, Discriminant Analysis and the Prediction of Corporate Bankruptcy." *Journal of Finance* (September).

————. 1971. *Corporate Bankruptcy in America*. Lexington: Heath Lexington.

————. 1973. "Predicting Railroad Bankruptcies in America." *Bell Journal of Economics and Management Science* (Spring).

————. 1983. *Corporate Financial Distress*. New York: John Wiley & Sons.

————. 1990. *Investing in Distressed Securities*. Los Angeles: The Foothill Group, Inc.

————. 1991. *Distressed Securities*. Chicago: Probus Publishing Co.

Altman, E. and M. Fridson. 1990. "An Introduction to the Altman-Merrill Index of Defaulted Securities." *Extra Credit* (November): 10-16.

Altman, E., R. Haldeman, and P. Narayanan. 1977. "Zeta Analysis: A New Model to Identify Bankruptcy Risk of Corporations." *Journal of Banking and Finance* (June): 29-54.

Aziz, A. and G.H. Lawson. 1989. "Cash Flow Reporting and Financial Distress Models: Testing of Hypotheses." *Financial Management* (Spring): 55-63.

Beaver, W. 1966. "Financial Ratios as Predictors of Failure." *Empirical Research in Accounting: Selected Studies*. Supplement to *Journal of Accounting Research* 4.

————. 1968a. "Alternative Financial Ratios as Predictions of Failure." *The Accounting Review* (January).

————. 1968b. "Market Prices, Financial Ratios and the Predictions of Failure." *Journal of Accounting Research* (Autumn).

Bernstein, R. 1990. "Quantitative Viewpoint." Merrill Lynch & Co. Global Securities Research & Economics Group (December).

Blum, M. 1974. "Failing Company Discriminant Analysis." *Journal of Accounting Research* (Spring).

Casey, C. and N. Bartczak. 1984. "Cash Flow—It's Not the Bottom Line." *Harvard Business Review* (July-August): 36-49.

————. 1985. "Using Operating Cash Flow Data to Predict Financial Distress: Some Extensions." *Journal of Accounting Research* (Spring): 384-401.

Chen, K.H. and T.A. Shimerda. 1981. "An Empirical Analysis of Useful Ratios." *Financial Management* (Spring): 51-60.

Cottle, S., R.F. Murray, and F.E. Block. 1988. *Graham and Dodd's Security Analysis*, Fifth Edition. New York: McGraw-Hill Book Company.

Dambolena, I.G. and S.J. Khoury. 1980. "Ratio Stability and Corporate Failure." *Journal of Finance* (September): 1,107-26.

Dambolena, I.G. and J.M. Shulman. 1988. "A Primary Rule for Detecting Bankruptcy: Watch the Cash." *Financial Analysts Journal* (September/October): 74-78.

Deakin, E.B. 1972. "A Discriminant Analysis of Predictors of Business Failure." *Journal of Accounting Research* (Spring).

Edmister, R.O. 1972. "An Empirical Test of Financial Ratio Analysis for Small Business Failure Prediction." *Journal of Financial and Quantitative Analysis* (March).

Elam, R. 1975. "The Effect of Lease Data on the Predictive Ability of Financial Ratios." *Accounting Review* (January): 25-43.

Gentry, J.A., P. Newbold, and D.T. Whitford. 1984. "Bankruptcy, Working Capital and Funds Flow." *Managerial Finance* 10: 12-25.

Gentry, J.A., P. Newbold, and D.T. Whitford. 1985a. "Classifying Bankrupt Firms with Funds Flow Components." *Journal of Accounting Research* (Spring): 146-60.

————. 1985b. "Predicting Bankruptcy: If Cash Flow is Not the Bottom Line, What Is?" *Financial Analysts Journal* (September/October): 47-56.

Gombola, M.F., M.E. Haskins, J.E. Katz, and D.D. Williams. 1987. "Cash Flow in Bankruptcy Prediction." *Financial Management* (Winter): 55-65.

Helfert, Eric. 1982. *Techniques of Financial Analysis.* Homewood, Ill.: Richard D. Irwin, Inc.

Hickman, W.B. 1958. *Corporate Bond Quality and Investors Experience.* Princeton: Princeton University Press and the National Bureau of Economic Research.

Hradsky, G. and R. Long. 1989. "High Yield Losses and the Return Performance of Bankrupt Debt Issuers: 1978-1988." *Financial Analysts Journal* (July/August): 38-49.

Largay, J.A. and C.P. Stickney. 1980. "Cash Flows, Ratio Analysis and the W.T. Grant Company Bankruptcy." *Financial Analysts Journal* (July/August): 51-54.

Libby, R. 1975. "Accounting Ratios and the Prediction of Failure: Some Behavioral Evidence." *Journal of Accounting Research* (Spring).

Loque, D.E., ed. 1990. *Handbook of Modern Finance,* Second Edition. Boston: Warren, Gorham & Lamont.

Menash, Y.M. 1983. "The Differential Bankruptcy Predictive Ability of Specific Price Level Adjustments: Some Empirical Evidence." *Accounting Review* (April): 228-46.

Moyer, R. 1977. "Forecasting Financial Failure: A Re-Examination." *Financial Management* (Spring).

Norton, C.L. and R.E. Smith. 1979. "A Comparison of General Price Level and Historical Cost Financial Statements in the Prediction of Bankruptcy." *The Accounting Review* (January): 72-87.

Ohlson, J.S. 1980. "Financial Ratios and the Probabilistic Prediction of Bankruptcy." *Journal of Accounting Research* (Spring): 109-31.

Scott, J. 1981. "The Probability of Bankruptcy: A Comparison of Empirical Predictions and Theoretical Models." *Journal of Banking and Finance* (September): 317-44.

Spiotto, J.E. 1990. *Defaulted Securities: The Prudent Indenture Trustee's Guide.* American Bankers Association.

Taffler, R. J. 1982. "Forecasting Company Failure in the U.K. Using Discriminant Analysts and Financial Ratio Data." *Journal of Royal Statistical Society* 145, Part 3: 342-58

Tamari, M. 1966. "Financial Ratios as a Means of Forecasting Bankruptcy." *Management International Review* 4 (15-21).

Werbalowsky, J.I. and C.J. Stanford. 1989. *Deleveraging the Troubled Company.* Los Angeles: Houlihan, Lokey, Howard & Zukin Capital.

Wilcox, J.W. 1971. "A Simple theory of Financial Ratios as Predictors of Failures." *Journal of Accounting Research* (Autumn): 389-95.

Wilcox, J. 1973. "A Prediction of Business Failure Using Accounting Data." *Empirical Research in Accounting: Selected Studies.* Supplement to *Journal of Accounting Research.*

Zavgren, C. 1983. "The Prediction of Corporate Failure: The State of the Art." *Journal of Accounting Literature* (Spring): 1-38.

Self-Evaluation Examination

1. A company does not need to be insolvent to obtain bankruptcy protection, it merely has to be financially distressed.
    a. True.
    b. False.

2. Insolvency exists when:
    a. A company cannot pay debts as they become due.
    b. Liabilities exceed assets.
    c. Lawsuits cause a company to be unable to pay maturing debts.
    d. All of the above.

3. In a restructuring plan as opposed to a reorganization plan:
    a. The restructuring occurs outside of court.
    b. The plan can be approved if two-thirds of the creditors agree to it.
    c. The plan can be approved if the largest class of creditor accepts the plan.
    d. None of the above.

4. Empirical research indicates that net operating cash flow is an important predictor of bankruptcy.
    a. True.
    b. False.

5. All of the following variables were found to be important in the cash flow bankruptcy prediction models [Gentry, Newbold, and Whitford (1985 a,b)] *except*:
    a. Investment.
    b. Dividends.
    c. Fixed charge coverage ratio.
    d. Accounts receivable.

6. In his summary of bankruptcy prediction models, Reilly concludes that:
    a. Cash flow models are more useful to investors attempting to predict bankruptcy than financial ratio models.
    b. Financial ratio models are more useful to investors attempting to predict bankruptcy than cash flow models.
    c. Both cash flow and financial ratio models are useful to investors attempting to predict bankruptcy.
    d. Neither cash flow nor financial ratio models are useful to investors interested in attempting to predict bankruptcy.

7. The most useful financial ratios for predicting failure are:
    a. Financial leverage ratios.
    b. Receivables turnover ratios.
    c. Profitability ratios.
    d. All of the above.

8. According to Wilson, bond covenants no longer work.
    a. True.
    b. False.

9. The three C's of credit are:
    a. Collateral, covenants, and character.
    b. Character, costs, and collateral.
    c. Collateral, covenants, and capacity.
    d. Character, capacity, and collateral.

10. Altman estimates that the size of the privately traded defaulted and distressed debt market is about the same size as the publicly traded defaulted and distressed debt market.
    a. True.
    b. False.

11. Because of the risky nature of investing in defaulted and distressed securities, investors require minimum rates of return:
    a. In the range of 20 to 30 percent.
    b. In the range of 15 to 20 percent.
    c. Greater than 13 percent.
    d. Greater than 16 percent.

12. According to Altman, the best time to buy distressed securities is:
    a. One year before bankruptcy.
    b. Six months before bankruptcy.
    c. At the announcement of bankruptcy.
    d. Six months after bankruptcy.

13. According to Levy, the key to success with active approaches to investing in distressed securities is:
    a. To avoid becoming restricted.
    b. To buy securities after the bankruptcy is announced.
    c. The ability to influence the affairs of the company on a day-to-day basis.
    d. All of the above.

14. An investor would become restricted if:
    a. He received nonpublic information.
    b. He purchased more than 10 percent of the equity.
    c. He owned securities at the time a reorganization is announced.
    d. All of the above.

15. The advantage of buying privately issued debt versus publicly issued debt in the distressed firm market is:
    a. Private debt is usually higher in the capital structure than public debt.
    b. Private debt can often be purchased more easily.
    c. Both of the above.
    d. Neither of the above.

16. Investing in distressed securities is not the same in international markets as it is in the United States, primarily because the absolute priority rule is followed in international markets.
    a. True.
    b. False.

17. Which of the following factors affect the value of senior secured debt:
    a. Lender liability risk.
    b. Equitable subordination risk.
    c. Fraudulent conveyance risk.
    d. All of the above.

18. According to Breazzano, the key to success versus failure in investing in the securities of distressed and bankrupt firms is:
    a. To buy securities at the right price.
    b. To buy securities within six months of the bankruptcy announcement.
    c. To buy securities within six months after the bankruptcy announcement.
    d. To sell securities before the bankruptcy is announced.

19. According to Takahashi, reasons why the market for distressed securities might be undervalued include:
    a. Bankruptcy frightens many investors.
    b. The analysis of bankruptcies is quite complex.
    c. Many lenders and portfolio managers would rather sell debt at a huge discount than face uncertain resumption of payment.
    d. All of the above.

20. In many instances, returns to investments in defaulted bonds tend to be more dependent on deal-specific issues and the assets of the company rather than a market multiple and the company's future earnings.
    a. True.
    b. False.

Self-Evaluation Answers

1.   b.   See Spiotto (p. 3).

2.   d.   See Spiotto (pp. 3-4).

3.   a.   See Spiotto (p. 11).

4.   b.   See Gentry (p. 19).

5.   c.   See Gentry (p. 19).

6.   c.   See Reilly (p. 26).

7.   a.   See Reilly (p. 25).

8.   b.   See Wilson (p. 31).

9.   d.   See Wilson (p. 32).

10.   b.   See Altman (p. 36).

11.   a.   See Altman (p. 39).

12.   d.   See Altman (p. 39).

13.   c.   See Levy (p. 44).

14.   a.   See Greenhaus (p. 47).

15.   c.   See Levy and Greenhaus Question and Answer Session (p. 50).

16.   a.   See Levy and Greenhaus Question and Answer Session (p. 51).

17.   d.   See Werbalowsky (pp. 62-63).

18.   a.   See Breazzano (p. 65).

19.   d.   See Takahashi (p. 72).

20.   a.   See Takahashi (p. 73).